Marion Wright has worked for the Citizens Advice Bureau for over ten years, both as a volunteer and in her current position as Deputy Manager of the Norwich and District CAB.

She has also worked as a teacher, both in the United Kingdom and abroad. She is the author of *A Death in the Family* (Optima, 1987).

OPTIMA

YOUNG PEOPLE'S RIGHTS

MARION WRIGHT

An OPTIMA book

© Marion Wright

First published in 1990 by
Macdonald Optima, a division of
Macdonald & Co. (Publishers) Ltd

A Member of Maxwell Macmillan Pergamon Publishing Corporation

British Library Cataloguing in Publication Data
Wright, Marion
   Young people's rights.
   1. England. Young persons.
   I. Title
   344.202'87

ISBN 0-356-15989-2

Macdonald & Co (Publishers) Ltd
Orbit House
1 New Fetter Lane
London EC4A 1AR

Typeset in Century Schoolbook by Leaper & Gard Ltd, Bristol

Printed and bound in Great Britain by
The Guernsey Press Co. Ltd, Guernsey, Channel Islands

CONTENTS

FOREWORD

This book has been written to help young people under 18 try and find their way through the maze of legislation that affects them. One of the difficulties of living in this country is sorting out when you are or are not allowed to do something by law and when it is a matter of negotiation with parents, teachers, employers or friends.

Sometimes situations are straightforward. Sometimes a piece of legislation is not aimed at young people directly but it may still have an effect on their lives. For example, when parents are divorcing, how do young people make sure that their point of view is taken into account. Do they have a right to say what should happen to them?

So, as well as trying to answer questions about school uniform, pocket money, cheap travel, etc., this book sets out what should happen when you start work, want to marry, go into care, have contact with the police, want to leave home, and what consideration should be given to young people when parents divorce or remarry.

In deciding what information to include I have been helped by the students of the Hewett School, Norwich. Discussion with them of the bewildering number of rights and responsibilities thrust upon them has helped me to decide what should be included in this book. For their assistance I am most grateful.

SCOTTISH LAW

Because of the tremendous differences between the law in England and Scotland, the most obvious being the difference in the age of majority – 16 in Scotland, 18 in England & Wales, all references relate to English law and not Scottish. Where Scottish references are made it is to emphasise these differences.

1.
WHILE YOU ARE LIVING AT HOME

Since I got a job last summer my young sister, she's 12, has been on and on at my mum and dad to let her have a job. Our next door neighbour has said she will pay her to look after her little boy while she goes late night shopping once a week. Can she babysit when she's 12?

BABYSITTING OR BEING LEFT ALONE

There is nothing in law which states an age at which a child can be left with a babysitter or how old that babysitter should be. It makes no difference whether the babysitter is being paid or not.

Where the police or social services may become involved is when they are told that a child is being left alone continuously, or there is an accident while the parents are absent, for example if there were a fire. In extreme circumstances care proceedings may follow. There is also the situation where if a babysitter who was over 16, allowed any child under 12 years of age that they were looking after to be in a room where there was an unguarded fire and the child was injured, then the young person themself would be guilty of an offence. This would be in addition to any prosecution of the parents of the young child.

So, if a young person wants to babysit and the parents are satisfied that they are sensible then they are not breaking the law by letting them babysit or by paying them — but see Chapter 4, 'When you want to get a job'.

CHANGING YOUR NAME

Only your parents can apply to change your surname while you are under 16. If your natural parents are divorced and one of them has remarried, they will probably have to apply to court to change your surname to the new family name. When you reach the age of 16 you can change your surname if your parents consent.

If you have been christened or baptised you will not be able to change these Christian or forenames, but there is nothing to stop you using another forename if you can persuade everyone else to use it.

DRINKING ALCOHOL IN PRIVATE

You are not allowed to drink alcohol under the age of 5, unless you are given it for medical reasons. From then until you are 16 years old you can drink alcohol on private premises, for example at home.

For rules about buying and drinking alcohol in pubs and restaurants see Chapter 8, page 116.

EAR PIERCING AND HAIRSTYLES

If you want to have your ears pierced or your hair cut or styled in a particular way then there is nothing in law to stop you. But if your parents don't like the result they can argue that you were not old enough to appreciate what you were doing – you were not capable of consenting to the service. It is generally accepted that:

1. If you are under 10 you are not capable of giving consent.
2. Between the ages of 10 and 14 you are thought capable once you have had the implications of what you are doing explained to you.
3. Once you are 14 you are felt to be capable of giving consent in these particular circumstances.

You will find that ear piercing services are well aware of these rough guidelines, and so will not pierce your ears unless one of your parents is present and signs a consent form, and hairdressers may want to check with your parents if they are not happy about you making the hairdressing appointment.

FIREWORKS

You should not be sold or try to buy fireworks under the age of 16. Shopkeepers can be prosecuted if they agree to sell you fireworks while you are younger.

GUNS AND OTHER WEAPONS

1. If you are under the age of 14 you may not own, buy or be lent any kind of firearm or hold a firearms certificate. However, you may be allowed to use guns if you are a member of a shooting club.
2. Once you are 14 years of age you may own or borrow an airgun, but you are still not allowed to buy or hire a gun.
3. While you are under 15 years of age you should not be given a shotgun and you may only handle one if there is someone to supervise you and that person is over 21 years of age.
4. Once you are 17 years of age you can buy, hire and obtain a licence for any sort of firearm. You may also buy or hire a crossbow.

HORSERIDING

You will be allowed to hire a horse if there is someone to supervise you whilst you ride and that person is over 16 years of age.

NEGLIGENCE OR DAMAGE THAT YOU MAY CAUSE

You are negligent if you fail to take reasonable care and cause damage to someone else or their property. An example of this would be if you fell off your bicycle and damaged someone else's car or caused them to have an accident.

You can be held liable for your own negligence while you are under 18 years of age and you can be sued via your parents. However there would be no point in suing you if you have no money, and the court would take your age into account when deciding if you were negligent. So it may be that your parents would be sued directly. They are not liable for your negligence, but they can themselves be held to be negligent if they fail to supervise you and your activities properly.

PETS

You can own a pet at any age, but you must be 12 years of age before you are allowed to buy one, unless one of your parents is present.

PHYSICAL PUNISHMENT

Parents have a legal right to punish their children, and this includes smacking them – corporal punishment. However, if they are too severe parents can be charged with assault and the child or young person concerned may be taken into care – see Chapter 3, page 42.

POCKET MONEY

There are no laws relating to the payment of pocket money. It is entirely a matter of negotiation with your parents.

RELIGIOUS UPBRINGING

If your parents decide to have you christened or baptised or made a member of a particular faith while you are young there is no law to stop them. While you live with them they can insist that you be taught about their religion. If your parents disagree about your religious upbringing then they can ask a court to decide.

2.
WHEN YOU GO TO SCHOOL

My mum has just bought me a blouse in a sale. She says it is almost the same as the one I'm supposed to have for school but she didn't buy it in the shop the school recommends. Can I be sent home if I wear it for school?

DO YOU HAVE TO GO TO SCHOOL?

Parents, or whoever is legally responsible for you, have a legal duty to see that you receive full-time education between the ages of 5 and 16. It does not have to be at school. If your parents can convince the local education authority (LEA) that they can educate you without sending you to school then they will be allowed to do so. They will have to show that the education would be 'efficient, full-time and suitable'. (See Useful addresses for helpful organisations.)

WHEN DO YOU START?

Some LEAs provide education for under-fives, with pre-school and nursery facilities, but they do not have to provide a full-time place in a school until the term after a child reaches its fifth birthday. The exception is where a child has special needs (see page 19).

Some schools will admit children under this age for part of the day or for one or two days a week, but this will depend on the space in each school.

CHOOSING A SCHOOL

Your parents have some rights when it comes to choosing a school. Hopefully they would consult you and take your preferences into account, particularly when it comes to selecting a secondary school. Schools are now obliged to publish information books about themselves, which will include information about the organisation of the school, subjects that they can offer, exam results where this is appropriate, homework policy, discipline, etc. Parents can express a preference for a certain primary or secondary school; you must be allowed to go there unless the school and the LEA decide that there isn't enough room, or it is a grammar school or city technology college and the education offered isn't suitable for you.

After September 1990 all secondary schools will have a standard number of pupils and a policy of open enrolment. This means that if there is a place in the school you will be able to go there – the LEA will not be able to spread numbers of children throughout the local schools, as they have done in the past. Open enrolment may eventually be extended to the selection of primary schools. This means that if a school is popular there will be more applications than there are places. Schools will then have to decide which children have preference because they live near the school, have brothers and sisters already at the school, or there are good medical or social reasons for a child to go to that school.

If you are not given a place at your chosen school you will be offered a place at another one. If your parents don't like this decision they can appeal to a local appeals committee. If this committee agrees with your parents then you must be allowed to go to the chosen school.

If your parents choose to send you to a private school, then they will have to pay fees, unless they qualify for help under the Assisted Places Scheme. If they wish to send you to a city technology college then you will be assessed to see if you are suitable.

PROBLEMS WHILE AT SCHOOL

Who makes the rules?

School rules are decided by the governors of a school and the headteacher. The rules have to be 'reasonable', yet there is no legal basis for what is reasonable. You and your parents should have a good idea what some of the school's attitudes are before you get there, as school policy should be clearly set out in the school's information booklet.

Choice of subjects

The 1988 Education Act established a National Curriculum to make sure that you receive a balanced and broad education which is relevant to your needs. The National Curriculum consists of:

1. Three core subjects – English, mathematics and science.
2. Seven other foundation subjects – history, geography, technology, modern languages in secondary schools, art, music and physical education.
3. Religious education must be provided for all pupils.

When it is time for you to choose your GCSE options at 14 you may not be able to take a particular subject because it does not fit into the school's timetable. You have no legal right to be consulted about the structure of the timetable, but any good school will discuss your choices with you and should take your wishes into consideration.

Schools are not allowed by law to prevent you from taking a particular subject because of your sex, so girls cannot be prevented from studying woodwork or electronics or boys from choosing home economics.

Examinations

At GCSE and A level the school will apply to the local examination board on your behalf and enter you for your chosen subject if they feel it is worth your while to sit the exam. If you or your parents want you to take an additional subject you may be able to enter externally by applying directly to the local examination board. You will find the appropriate address in the *Education Yearbook* (see page 127).

If you think that the school is discriminating against you or acting unreasonably, you or your parents should complain (see page 25). If it is your parents who are preventing you from taking a particular subject, try discussing the situation with the teacher involved, the head of department or the headteacher. This can also help if you are having problems choosing subjects to take at GCSE and A level.

Homework

Most secondary schools and some primary schools set homework – the school's policy will be set out in the school's handbook. Primary schools cannot insist that a child does homework, although it will argue, particularly with older children, that it encourages self discipline in work practices, i.e. looking up information for a project, and it is good preparation for secondary school.

At secondary school it is reasonable and expected that you will do some homework. You should have a timetable, and if you are working too late at night and at weekends then you and your parents should discuss this with the school.

But there is nothing in law to say that homework is compulsory. It is a matter of agreement between you, your parents and the school. Some schools may make homework a condition of being entered for an examination; indeed, some GCSE syllabuses now include homework assignments which count towards the final grade. However, the legality of this has yet to be tested in court.

Religious education

All schools must provide religious education for their pupils as part of the basic curriculum. State schools also have to provide a daily act of collective worship of a mainly Christian content. You have a right to withdraw from both religious studies and the act of worship if you wish. If you are of a faith other than Christianity then your parents can ask for you to receive instruction in your faith, and the LEA should provide facilities.

The part played by both the Anglican and the nonconformist churches in British education is an historic one; hence the presence of religious education as part of the curriculum, unlike other countries such as the USA where religious education is absent from school timetables. Many people, not just those of minority faiths but also humanists and atheists, feel discriminated against in schools. Many schools will find the insistence on an act of worship with a mainly Christian content in conflict with the aim of promoting a sense of community within the school.

Other subjects

Two areas of study that can cause difficulty in school are sex education and politics.

Governing bodies of schools decide the content of sex education in schools. This includes information about contraception and AIDS. They have to make sure that sex education is given 'in such a manner as to encourage pupils to have due regard to moral considerations and the value of family life'. Parents can ask to have their children withdrawn from lessons, but they have no right to insist on this. If you disagree with your parents withdrawing you from these lessons, try and get help from another member of your family or the school.

Schools are not allowed to present any information that could be argued is biased or one-sided, and this applies equally to party politics, nuclear or conventional defence, abortion, conservation issues, blood sports, etc. If you think that one point of view is being put forward to the exclusion of others then you should complain either through your school council or to the governing body.

Uniform

There is no law saying that you must wear school uniform. However, headteachers are allowed to say what they consider reasonable clothing for school; they might not let you wear jeans or heavy-duty boots, and pupils are often sent home if they are not being reasonable about what they are wearing. But it is perfectly reasonable for a parent to buy, say, a dress or shirt similar to the one asked for by the school, but in a different shop to the one recommended by the school, or in a sale. Most schools publish a list of school uniform or attire in their handbooks and a list of stockists and a price list.

Difficulties can arise if there is a no-trousers policy for girls and Hindu and Moslem girls wish to wear them for cultural and religious reasons; the school could be held to be racially discriminating against the girls by enforcing this rule. Similarly a Sikh boy should not be excluded from school because he wears a turban and keeps his hair long.

Most problems with dress are often to do with earrings, make up and too long or too short hair. Nowadays headteachers and governors adopt a more flexible attitude once pupils enter the fifth or sixth year. Indeed, some teachers feel that the policing element present in enforcing school uniform takes up valuable teaching time and can prove disruptive to the fostering of good relationships between teacher and pupils, although others feel that uniform is important in enforcing discipline and the identity of the school.

Some LEAs may be able to help with school uniform, but they are not obliged by law to do this. The help may be in the form of cash or vouchers to spend in certain shops. The school may organise the grant applications, so ask either the school secretary or a senior member of staff. If your LEA does not do this or has run out of money for uniforms when you need it, try the school or parent teacher association (PTA) who often have secondhand clothes for sale. Your local Citizen's Advice Bureau should know about local charities who provide money for educational needs.

Attendance and truancy

If you are away from school for a day or two because you are ill, then a note to the school from your parents or doctor will be all right. You may also be away from school for two weeks for a holiday during school time or away on a particular day to attend a religious observance, provided you have obtained permission from the school.

But if you continue to be away from school without the knowledge or consent of the school, they may decide that you are playing truant. The school will contact your parents, either by letter or telephone, and try to sort the matter out. If this fails the school will inform the educational welfare officer (EWO), who will visit your home. If you continue to stay away from school the EWO will warn your parents that court action may follow if you don't go to school. Your parents may then be prosecuted in a magistrates court for failing to send you for school. If the truancy continues the LEA may apply to the juvenile court to ask for you to be taken into care, or may suggest that you be transferred to a special unit in another school. However your parents should only accept this suggestion if they feel that it is best for you.

Bullying, racial and sexual discrimination, and harassment

One of the reasons that people play truant is because they are being bullied or harassed or discriminated against in some way. You may not feel like talking about any of these things with your teachers, or it may be that the particular form of discrimination is actually being carried out by a member of staff. In all these cases you must talk it over with your parents and find a teacher or a senior member of staff to listen to you. They should try to enlist the help of community, race relations or women's groups to support you, particularly if the school seems unable to do anything.

Some schools have clearly developed anti-racist policies, and some LEAs have special advisors to whom you can speak and ask for advice. You also have the chance to appeal to the governors, the LEA and the Secretary of State for Education. In the case of a physical assault where the reason is obviously racial, then the police should also be informed.

Detention and other forms of punishment

If your school uses detention as a form of punishment, this should be made clear in the school's information book, and your parents should be given warning on any occasions when you are to be kept in detention. The school should not put you at risk by keeping you in detention; so, for example, you should not end up walking home in the dark alone after detention. If your parents do not want you to be kept in after school they should tell the school in writing. If you think that a detention is unreasonable your parents can complain to the school.

Corporal punishment (caning) was abolished in state schools on 15 August 1987, and it may not be used in private schools if the pupil is there because the fees are being paid under the Assisted Places Scheme. However, a teacher is able to act in self-defence, for example to break up a fight, or to stop someone hurting themselves or damaging school property. Other punishments that may be used by the school must be appropriate, i.e. extra work or loss of privileges.

Sent home from school

You may be sent home from school for various reasons other than discipline. For example, a school can send you home because you have an infectious disease which other people can catch, such as scabies or impetigo. In this case a school doctor will probably have examined you and they will tell your parents what treatment they advise for your illness. If your parents do not follow this treatment then they may be held to be not fulfilling their obligations to see that you get full-time education.

Suspension

If the suspension from school is for disciplinary reasons,

the only person who can authorise this is the headteacher, who must inform your parents, or you if you are over 18, of the reasons for suspension. The letter should make clear:

1. Why you have been suspended.
2. How long the suspension is to last, i.e. for a fixed term or an indefinite period.
3. Your parents' right to appeal to the governors or the LEA.

If you have been suspended for more than five days in any one term, or you will miss an important exam such as GCSE or A levels, then the headteacher must tell both the governing body and the LEA why you have been suspended, and for how long.

If you have been suspended, your parents should try and arrange a meeting with the headteacher as soon as possible. They can take someone with them for support if they wish – a friend, a member of the PTA or a parent governor, for example.

If your school does not offer a formal appeal hearing to the governing body, then your parents should write to the governors putting the case to have your suspension lifted. The governors are bound to take notice of your letter. If they do agree to meet you, then your parents should find out what form the hearing will take, how formal it will be, will they be given a chance to present your side of the case, and they should try and get someone to go with them.

If the governors decide in your favour, i.e. that you should not be suspended, then the headteacher is obliged to reinstate you if you have been suspended for more than five days. If you remain suspended you may then be able to appeal to the LEA and also the Secretary of State for Education. And if you do remain suspended the LEA still has a responsibility to provide you with education for at least a minimum of 10 hours a week, which can include course work for examinations.

Expulsion

Only a headteacher can expel a pupil. Again the head must inform your parents, and they should have an opportunity to discuss the matter with him/her and the chance to appeal to the governing body, the LEA and the Secretary of State. If the appeal fails the LEA must still provide you with education, and may offer the alternatives of transfer to another school in the area, following an assessment of your educational needs, or transfer to a special school. Your parents should be involved in these choices and they may need to seek advice and support from other groups interested in education and young people generally.

School files

All schools keep files on pupils throughout their time at school. At present neither you nor your parents have any legal right to see your files, although many schools and LEAs have adopted a policy of allowing parents to see pupil files. If you do see your file and find that some inaccurate information has been included, then you should complain and try to get it removed. Schools use these files to assess pupils when they first arrive at a new school and when they leave, for example when giving references to an employer or college or university.

School reports tend to be shown to both parents and pupils unless the school has a strict policy of not letting pupils see reports. If this is the case then it is up to you to discuss the matter with your parents.

If you have been assessed as having special educational needs then your parents do have a right to have a copy of the report and all the advice suggested.

Damage to you, your property or to the school

If you have an accident at school it must be recorded. During visits out of school, for example to a museum or swimming pool, a teacher is in the same position as your parents when they are in charge of you, unless your parents disagree. This is called acting *in loco parentis*. If you suffer a serious injury and your parents feel that the LEA is at fault, then they should take advice from a solicitor and seek the support of the PTA in a possible claim for negligence.

Your parents may consider it worthwhile to take out insurance to cover you while you are at school, especially if they find that the LEA have limited cover for accidents. A school is under no obligation to provide insurance against accidents in school. (See page 12 for details of accident insurance at school.)

If you do any damage at school you can be asked to pay for the repairs. The only way the school could force you to pay would be by taking you to court, or they might ask your parents to pay or take them to court.

A school should provide facilities for storing and drying pupils' outdoor clothing and for storing their other belongings. And once young people are over the age of 16 there should also be space for them for private study and social purposes.

School meals

A school meal no longer has to be of nutritional value. Many schools, especially secondary schools, now operate a cafeteria system, where pupils can choose from hot and cold meals and drinks. Parents whose children follow special diets for health or religious reasons should make sure that the school does consider this when drawing up menus. If parents or pupils feel that they are being discriminated against, then as a group they should complain to the school and the LEA.

The only pupils eligible for free school meals are those whose parents are claiming income support – everyone else has to pay. Because of this, and because many parents and pupils think that the school meals no longer provide value for money, there has been a large increase in the number of pupils taking packed lunches to school. The school should therefore provide somewhere inside the school building for pupils to eat packed lunches.

School milk

LEAs no longer have to provide milk free of charge to
pupils, but they can provide it and charge. LEAs may
provide milk for special groups, i.e. under sevens, so it is
worth finding out if your LEA does this. Children of
income support claimants may get free milk if the LEA
treats milk as part of the free school meal.

Transport

You may get help with fares to and from school if you live
beyond a certain distance. If you are under eight and live
more than two miles from school, or over eight and live
more than three miles from school, you should get help.
These distances are considered to be reasonable walking
distances, and are measured by the nearest available
route, which will not necessarily be the safest route – an
available route has been held to be a safe route for an
accompanied child, not an unaccompanied child.
However, if you have gone to a school of your choice and
there is another suitable school nearer to you, the LEA
would not feel obliged to pay your fares.

Pupils who are disabled would normally qualify for free
transport. Parents visiting their children in a special
school may get all or part of their fares refunded. It would
be helpful in these circumstances to get a letter from a
doctor or social worker.

School trips and visits

Changes brought in by the 1988 Education Act have
meant that the policy of charging for activities and trips
organised by schools has altered. The general rule is that if
an activity takes place in school time or is a necessary
part of a course being followed by a pupil, the school
cannot charge, only ask for a voluntary donation to cover
costs. Schools are therefore likely to see what voluntary
contributions would be available before making a decision
about a trip or visit. However, once a decision is made to
go then heads are not allowed to discriminate when
choosing young people to take part. Where parents receive

income support or family credit, schools can have any costs that they incur for board and lodging rebated by the LEA.

Schools are obliged to publish a statement of their policy concerning charges for activities in its information booklet, so that you can check before you decide whether or not to go there.

RESPONSIBILITIES OF THE LEA TO PROVIDE EDUCATION

If you are in care

Young people in care have the same rights to education as anyone else. In addition the social services department which has responsibility for you has a duty to consult you when making decisions and to take account of your views.

If you are in voluntary care your parents will still make choices about your education, hopefully having consulted you first. If you are living with foster parents, having been placed there by social services, then your foster parents make the decisions, but social services still have a duty to consult you.

If you are in care there is no reason for the school to let it be generally known. If it becomes general knowledge and you don't like it you should talk to your social worker and consider complaining to the school.

If you are ill

If you are going to be away from school for a long time because you are ill, get your parents to arrange with the school to have work sent home. You have the right to education while you are at home.

If you go into hospital the LEA is still responsible for providing you with education. If it is only to be a short period in hospital, followed by convalescence at home, then the arrangements described above for illness at home apply. If you are going to be in hospital for a long time then you have the right to be educated while you are in hospital. Your parents should find out what the LEA and the hospital are prepared to provide. Very often teachers – not just those from your school – are available while you are in hospital.

If you are pregnant

Being pregnant should not stop you receiving education. Some schools or LEAs may try to encourage or tell you to leave, but unless your doctor says you cannot go to school for medical reasons you should be allowed to go and you should complain to the LEA about any attempt made to exclude you. If you must be taught at home then the LEA or the school should provide you with work or a home tutor.

If you do decide to go to school then you should check with your doctor about any additional care you should take. The doctor can advise you or speak to the local Health and Safety Executive on your behalf. For example, concerns have been expressed about the long-term effect on pregnant women working with VDUs.

If you are still eligible to return to school after the baby is born you are entitled to expect the LEA to provide you with full-time education up to the age of 19, if you wish it. The LEA should help you make childcare arrangements while you are at school.

If you are in custody

If you are sent by the courts to any custodial institution, youth custody or detention centre you no longer have any rights to education as you would at school. However, if you are of school age, all penal institutions have rules concerning education, so you should be able to attend classes. The LEA have powers to provide you with education while you are serving your sentence.

If you have special needs

Difficulties with learning. Both primary and secondary schools should offer help to pupils who have difficulties with learning. This is often referred to as remedial education. In primary schools it may be that children will be given extra help either individually or as a group, often getting help with basic skills such as reading, writing and maths. Schools may get extra funds or an additional teacher for this work. Cuts in education funding mean that 'remedial education' has suffered but parents should insist, on your behalf, that you get help, if you need it. In secondary schools a remedial unit may operate separately or assist pupils who are more integrated within the school. *If English is not your first language.* If you need help with improving your English because it is not your first language the LEA must provide it. If you or your parents wish you to continue to develop your knowledge of your own 'mother tongue' and your school does not provide it then you should consider moving to another school. Some local authorities provide teaching within schools, some support community projects. But you have no 'right' to have lessons in your mother tongue.

If you need extra help with English your school should not put you into a separate unit within the school for all your work nor should the LEA insist that you should be educated in a special school. This form of separation because of language has been held to be discriminatory under the Race Relations Act.

If you have disabilities

Children, through their parents, can ask for an assessment of their need for special education between the ages of 2 and 19. The LEA should then assess you and give a copy of their recommendations to your parents. Children with disabilities are not just those who are severely handicapped or of low ability or blind or deaf, but often those with minor handicaps; the Warnock Committee in 1978 suggested that 20 per cent of children need special educational help at some point in their time at school. Like remedial education, help can be provided in different ways – in the class with other children, in a special unit in an ordinary school, or in a special school. Many young people who would have in the past been taught in special schools are now integrated into ordinary schools.

Statementing is the process of assessment carried out by the local authority, either because the parents have asked for it or the LEA think it necessary. A child will be examined and 'statements', i.e. written reports, will be made by a school doctor, an educational psychologist, the social services and the school. Your parents should be asked to give their views, and also have the right to be present at any examinations that take place. Any proposals that the LEA suggest should be discussed with your parents before any decisions are made. For parents, there is the right of appeal to the LEA and the Secretary of State for Education.

One of the main problems with statementing is that the procedure often takes a long time, sometimes over a year. If there are delays your parents should consider approaching your school governors to see if they will write to the LEA on your behalf.

LEAVING SCHOOL AT 16

Once you reach 16 you can leave school, but it does depend when your 16th birthday falls. If your birthday comes between 1 September and 31 January, then you cannot leave before the last day of the Easter term that follows your birthday. If your birthday is between 1 February and 31 August you may leave on the Friday before the last Monday in May. If you are taking exams the school will want you to stay on until the end of the summer term.

Careers advice at 16

If you decide that you are going to leave school when you are 16, then the LEA, through the school, has a duty to provide you with help and advice about finding a job or suitable training. The school will have some details printed in their handbook, together with the names of teachers responsible for coordinating and providing careers advice within the school.

If you feel the school isn't doing enough you can always

visit your local careers office – look them up under
'Careers advice' in the Yellow Pages.

Records of achievement at 16
Schools send reports to parents of pupils' work at regular
intervals during their time at school, although often these
only include exam results and attendance records.
However, by 1990 all school leavers will receive a record of
achievement, which will contain information of your other
achievements at school, your development of social and
practical skills and not just academic results.

EDUCATION AT 16+

Choosing what to do next
The choice of what to do lies between:

1. Leaving school and getting a job or some kind of
    training.
2. Staying on in the sixth form.
3. Going to a sixth form college.
4. Going to a college of further education.

Your decision should be based on what is best for you,
what you want to do and what qualifications you need.
   If you leave school but do not get a job you will not be
able to sign on as unemployed and draw benefits because
everyone between 16 and 18 not at school is guaranteed a
place on the Youth Training Scheme. (See Youth Training
Scheme, page 61, Income Support, page 100, and Housing
benefit, page 96.)

If you want to carry on studying
Any young person has the right to full-time education up
to their 19th birthday, and this includes people who are
mentally or physically handicapped. Full-time education
can be either at school or in a college. For people with a
physical or mental handicap it is not enough to provide
them with a place in an adult training centre; although

some of these centres have continuing education as part of their programmes, they do not count as full-time educational establishments.

You may decide to stay on at school – you have the right to do this. The difficulty may be that the school is unable to offer you the chance to take the subjects you want to study, or they may say that your grades at GCSE are not good enough for you to have a place in the sixth form, or for behavioural reasons the school is not prepared to let you stay on. If you or your parents cannot settle the matter by negotiation with the school it is worth seeing if another school in the area can give you a place to take the subjects that you want or the opportunity to re-take GCSEs.

Alternatively you may be able to go to a local sixth form college or college of further education. The main difference between sixth form at school, a sixth form college and a college of further education is that the FE college expects the student to take responsibility for turning up to lectures and handing in work on time while the school and the sixth form college will still retain many of the rules and classroom atmosphere that the student may be keen to get away from.

Fees while still in full-time education

While you are still in full-time education your parents or whoever looks after you can continue to receive child benefit for you; this can go on up to your 19th birthday, provided you are classified as still in full-time non-advanced education.

You will not have to pay fees to stay on in the sixth form at school or in sixth form college. As a rule LEAs do not charge for courses of non-advanced education, but in some areas there are already departures from this rule in colleges of further education for part-time students and evening classes. You will also probably have to pay fees if you decide to go to a college which is outside your LEA area.

If it is not clear what your LEA's policy is, or you are

not clear what is the best for you, then find out while you are still in the fifth year. Check:

1. Your school:
   - Which subjects you can take at A level.
   - How many GCSEs you need to enter the sixth form.
   - What chances there are for retaking GCSEs.
   - What chances there are for taking extra GCSEs.

2. Your local sixth form college or another secondary school in your area:
   - Number of GCSEs required for entry.
   - Possibilities for A levels and other courses.

3. College of further education:
   - Breadth of courses available, not just GCSEs and A levels.
   - Whether or not fees will be charged for full- and part-time courses.
   - Whether or not fees will be charged because you don't live in the immediate area.

For all three check for any extra costs, such as fares, equipment you may have to buy, new uniform you may need if you change schools, whether games are still compulsory.

Grants and maintenance allowances for non-advanced education

If you decide to go to a college of further education you can apply to your LEA for a grant. However any grant for non-advanced education, either part- or full-time, will be discretionary. (See Students and grants, page 104.)

If you decide to stay at school or go to a sixth form college for non-advanced education you can apply to the LEA for an educational maintenance allowance. These are also discretionary and means tested, which means that you or your parents will only qualify if you are very hard up.

Courses of non-advanced study include GCSEs, A level, Scottish Certificate O and Higher, OND, B/TEC national

diploma, Scotvec national certificate, Scottish certificate
of sixth form studies, foundation art courses, secretarial
courses with GCSE entry, NNEB, hairdressing courses.

MAKING A COMPLAINT

Trying to sort out a problem at school

If you are having problems at school it may not be
apparent to either your teachers or your parents. If you do
have difficulties with either your work or other people at
school, you or your parents can try to resolve it by
approaching the following people.

If it is to do with your work, try either your subject
teacher or the head of department. If it is a problem with
other people at school try to talk to the teacher in charge
of your year or a teacher you think you can trust. If you
don't think this is appropriate, or it doesn't work, try to
talk to one of the more senior members of staff; in a large
school there is likely to be not only a headteacher but a
number of deputy or assistant heads.

If the problem is not just yours but involves other
people, why not get together as a group and discuss how,
as a group, you are going to approach the school. If it is a
particular problem concerning discrimination or
harassment you may find it appropriate to take advice
from one of the organisations who assist with education
problems (see Useful addresses, page 121). As a group you
might be able to bring the matter to the attention of the
parent teacher association or the school council, if you
have one.

If these approaches fail to solve the problem then you
may want to approach the school governors. School
governors are either appointed or elected. Governing
bodies of schools are made up of people appointed by the
LEA, teacher governors elected by the teaching staff,
parent governors elected by the parents, and co-opted
governors, i.e. members of the community who are asked
to join the governing body by the existing governors. The
headteacher can also be a governor if they wish. You can

approach the governors if you have failed to resolve the problem with the staff. You might think that the best person to approach is one of the parent governors, but the parent governors are not delegates of parents and may feel inhibited about raising matters as they also have children at the school. However a good parent governor should be prepared to talk to both you and your parents and make enquiries about the difficulties that you may be having. It may be that your school has a more formal set-up, a proper appeals procedure, if you have a matter that you want to talk to the governors about. The school secretary will advise you how the procedure works.

Complaints against the implementation of the curriculum

From September 1989 parents and pupils will be able to complain if they feel that some aspect of the curriculum is not being correctly implemented. A complaint will be dealt with firstly by the head, then by the governors, then by a designated officer of the LEA, and finally by the Secretary of State for Education.

Getting help

If you or your parents are not happy about any appeals procedure set out by the LEA, discuss it with your local Citizen's Advice Bureau who have information about appeals, particularly schools selection appeals.

1. **The Secretary of State for Education.** If you feel that the LEA and school have acted unreasonably in carrying out one of their responsibilities, then you can approach the Secretary of State for Education. You go to him through your local MP or local councillors, either the councillor representing your area or a member of the local education committee. Your local Citizen's Advice Bureau will be able to tell you who the local councillors are and the address and the local surgery times of those councillors and your local MP.

2. **The Local Government Ombudsman** can
   investigate if you feel that your complaint has not been
   administered correctly, but the Ombudsman cannot
   deal with internal school problems or the decisions of
   an appeals committee.
3. **The European Court of Human Rights.** Having
   exhausted all these possibilities the final step is to
   appeal to the European Court of Human Rights. You
   would need legal advice, and legal aid may be
   available. Most recent cases have been about the use
   of corporal punishment (now abolished in state
   schools) and religious and sex education and other
   forms of discrimination. You will need the assistance
   of one of the education pressure groups. (For their
   names and addresses and the address of the European
   Court of Human Rights see Useful addresses.)

3. WHEN THINGS GO WRONG IN THE FAMILY

My mum and dad have been divorced for about five years. Last year my mum remarried. I've tried but I can't get on with my stepfather. Does he have the right to tell me off? Can he stop me going out at weekends? If my mum died, would he or my real dad be my guardian? I'm 16.

This chapter sets out what happens when things go wrong in a family. Often the remedies seem as painful as the situations that they are meant to ease. Very often, because the adults concerned are upset or angry, they may not be able or willing to let themselves be questioned or want to explain things to their children. However, in divorce, remarriage, adoption, fostering and care proceedings the overriding consideration of the law and the people responsible for administering it – the judge, registrar, social worker, court welfare officer – is to 'safeguard the interests of the child'.

What follows is an outline of what happens in these difficult situations and when young people should be consulted. All the words in this chapter in **bold type** are those used by solicitors and the courts.

DIVORCE AND SEPARATION

Separation
Many parents who decide to live apart may not want to divorce, merely to separate; for example, the religion of one or both of the parents may not allow them to divorce.

If they have never been married they can separate in an informal way. If they are married they can still live apart in an informal way, or have a **legal separation**. If this happens they will live apart while remaining married, but they will still have to make all the formal decisions that a couple who are divorcing have to make, such as where you are all going to live, what money there will be to live on and who is to be responsible for you.

Divorce

Your parents will not be able to get a divorce if they have been married for less than a year, and one of them must have been resident in England or Wales for at least a year when they do ask for the divorce. To be granted a divorce in England or Wales one of the partners in the marriage must show that **the marriage has irretrievably broken down.** They will prove that this has happened using one of the following reasons:

1. They have **lived apart for two years** and they **both** agree to a divorce.
2. One of them has committed **adultery**, i.e. has had sexual intercourse with another man or woman.
3. One of them has **behaved unreasonably** towards the other.
4. They have **lived apart for five years** and **one** of them wants a divorce.
5. One of your parents has **deserted** the other for at least **two years**.

In most divorce cases only one of your parents will file a **divorce petition**. This is called **undefended** divorce. If your other parent decides to object and enters a **cross petition** the case becomes **defended**. This is unusual because the defended divorces are very expensive and lengthy.

The parent who files the divorce petition is called the **petitioner**. Once the petition has been filed, i.e. sent to the divorce court, a copy will be sent to the **respondent** –

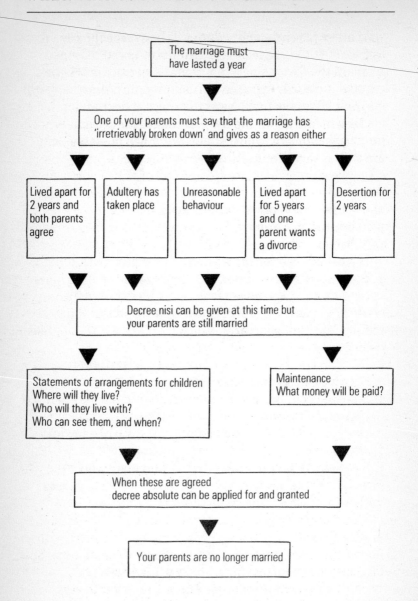

The marriage must have lasted a year

▼

One of your parents must say that the marriage has 'irretrievably broken down' and gives as a reason either

▼ ▼ ▼ ▼ ▼

| Lived apart for 2 years and both parents agree | Adultery has taken place | Unreasonable behaviour | Lived apart for 5 years and one parent wants a divorce | Desertion for 2 years |

▼ ▼ ▼ ▼ ▼

Decree nisi can be given at this time but your parents are still married

▼ ▼

Statements of arrangements for children
Where will they live?
Who will they live with?
Who can see them, and when?

Maintenance
What money will be paid?

▼ ▼

When these are agreed
decree absolute can be applied for and granted

▼

Your parents are no longer married

What happens during a divorce

your other parent – and a date will be set for the case to be heard. If the judge or registrar accepts the reasons given on the divorce petition then the petitioner will be granted a **decree nisi**. At this stage your parents are still married. The court will want to be satisfied that any disagreements about money – **maintenance**, and any property such as a house or a car or other possessions – have been sorted out. All these arrangements are collectively known as **ancillary relief**. The court will also want to know what arrangements have been made about the care of any children. A form called a **statement of arrangements** will have to be completed.

If all this is agreed, after six weeks the petitioner can apply for a **decree absolute**. However, if your parents cannot agree about arrangements for the children, the court may delay the grant of a decree absolute. Your parents will still be married until the decree absolute has been granted and issued by the court.

Arrangements for children

If you are very young when your parents divorce, then the decision about who you live with will be taken by your parents, unless the court who hears the divorce thinks that one or both of your parents would be unsuitable. But if the divorce happens when you are in your teens, the judge or registrar will make sure that your feelings and wishes are taken into consideration.

You may have good reason for wanting to live with one or other parent; for example you may get on better with one of them, or it may be that, because of the divorce, one of your parents is moving away from the area and, because of school work and friends, you want to stay where you are. The court should take all this into consideration when it makes a decision.

If your parents have decided between them what they want to do with you, you may find it difficult to let the court know if you want to do something else. You should try to discuss it with your parents, or get another adult such as a friend or relative to help you to put your point of view.

If your parents cannot decide or agree, then the court will usually ask for a **court welfare report**. A court welfare officer will talk to everyone involved and write a report for the court. If the court makes the decision, then you and your parents must abide by it. In order to speed up this process of reports the proposed parliamentary Children Bill says that there must be a timetable which the court and all the people involved must observe.

Of course, as you grow up situations and people change and you may want to go and live with your other parent. If you cannot get your parents to agree to this, then the case may go back to court, to ask the court to change the arrangements.

When your parents are married and when they are not married

Under existing legislation all the arrangements concerning who is responsible for looking after and making decisions for the children when a marriage breaks up are called **custody** or **care and control orders.** At present an unmarried mother has sole rights over her children, even if the couple have lived together for a number of years and the man recognises the children as his.

Under the proposed Children Bill care, custody and control orders will be replaced by **parental responsibility**. A married couple will automatically have parental responsibility, provided the court considers they are suitable. But the Bill proposes that an unmarried father will be able to have parental responsibility, either with the agreement of the mother or by asking a court. And other adults will be able to have parental responsibility if they are prepared to go to court.

Under the new Children Bill the types of arrangements concerning children will be called:

1. A **residence order**, which will decide where the children will live.

2. A **contact order** – who will be allowed to see the children and when this will happen.
3. A **specific issues order** – which parent will be able to make decisions for the child, for example choice of school or religious upbringing.
4. A **prohibited steps order** – this will clearly set out where parents may not make decisions concerning a child's welfare without the permission of the court.

Where a young person has reached the age of 17 these orders will apply in exceptional circumstances only.

In addition to parents, any adult with whom the child has been living for at least three years, including other children, can apply for parental responsibility, so aunts, uncles and grandparents or older children could apply.

Divorce and money

If your parents do not have very much money the cost of the divorce, that is seeing a solicitor, sending in the divorce petition, etc., can be met by legal aid (See Chapter 6). If one of your parents is earning they will have to pay part of their legal fees and the parent who is not earning will be helped by legal aid. If they are both earning they will probably both have to make a contribution to their own legal bills.

Whatever is decided, there is going to be a change in your living standards. The house that you are living in may have to be sold, even though the parent who looks after the children will normally have the right to stay in the house while the children are young. It could be part of the order made in the court that the other parent will have to move out and find somewhere else to live while still paying **maintenance,** that is a regular sum of money to the parent looking after the children. If the parent providing maintenance is the only one working this means that one wage packet may have to keep two homes going.

If there are children under the age of 16 living with the mother or father, the parent concerned will be able to claim income support from the Department of Social

Security (DSS) without having to sign on as available for work. This will help if there is very little money coming from the other parent. Income support can also cover some of the cost of a mortgage. If rent and rates have to be paid, then your mother or father, whoever looks after you, should apply to the local council to see if they can get any housing benefit.

If the parent that you are living with is working they may still be able to claim benefits. They can still apply for:

1. Housing benefit.
2. Family credit – a benefit specially designed for people with children who have low earnings.
3. One parent benefit, for people bringing up children on their own.

They should also check that their income tax is being deducted at the correct rate; parents bringing up children on their own are entitled to extra tax allowances, that is they can earn more money before income tax is deducted.

If you think that your parent may not be claiming, try and suggest that they check with their local welfare rights officer or Citizen's Advice Bureau.

REMARRIAGE AND STEP-PARENTS

Nearly 6 million people – adults and children – live in stepfamilies. A stepfamily is created when two partners decide either to live together or to marry and one or both of those partners has children from a previous relationship. You don't have to live together all the time to be a stepfamily. The National Stepfamily Association (see Useful addresses) includes stepfamilies who only come together for weekends or in the holidays.

A step-parent does not acquire automatic parental rights over the children in their new family. However, they will find that they will have some of the responsibilities of parents. For example a school may expect a step-parent to make sure that the children go to school.

A step-parent together with their partner assumes the responsibility of taking all the day-to-day decisions about the children in their care, but when it comes to major decisions such as which secondary school you will go to, which faith you will be brought up in, or changing your name, then the parent who has the custody or parental responsibility for you must take the decision. So it is likely that the two parents that you live with will present a united front when it comes to deciding about times for you to be in at the weekends.

A step-parent will only acquire the rights of a natural parent if they formally adopt their stepchildren. This means that even if the natural parent you live with dies, your step-parent will not automatically be your legal guardian. It is possible for the parent who has custody or parental responsibility for you to appoint your step-parent as your guardian if they die; the court can be asked to agree to this. But if your other natural parent objects, then it will be up to the court to decide what is in your best interests. In this situation your views should be sought.

If this relationship between your natural parent and step-parent breaks down and another divorce occurs, then providing your step-parent has adopted you as a **child of the family**, that is as part of the family, he or she will have the same rights and responsibilities as any other parent in a divorce. This is despite the fact that the natural father is still alive. If there has been no formal adoption there is no implied responsibility.

ADOPTION

Anyone who is under 18 and not married can be adopted. When a young person is adopted it means that all the parental responsibility passes to the adopting adult. An **adoption order** is drawn up by a court, and once the order is made it cannot be reversed – the young person's natural parents lose all their rights. (Fostering is not the

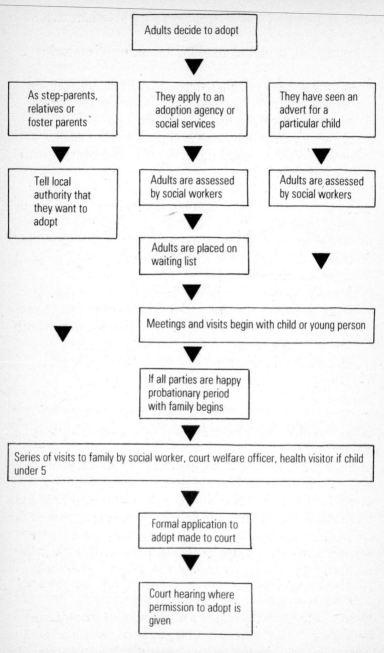

The route to adoption

same as adoption – see Care, page 42; Fostering, page 41.

Young people are adopted for a number of reasons:

1. A woman may decide before a child is born or at the time of the birth that she cannot care for the baby, and gives the baby up for adoption.
2. A young person has been in the care of the local authority for a long time and has had no contact with the natural parents.
3. A young person has been removed from their parents by the social services and is unlikely ever to be able to return home.
4. The young person's natural parents are divorced and one of the parents has remarried and the new couple wish to adopt the children.
5. A young person may be adopted by one of its blood relatives, e.g. aunt, grandparent. However, courts are reluctant to do this because of the severing of ties with the natural parents. The courts may consider guardianship, wardship or custodianship instead.
6. Both parents are dead.

Who decides who is suitable to be an adoptive parent

In most cases adoptions are arranged by an adoption agency, who often will be the local social services. The exception to this is where young people are being adopted by relatives, step-parents or private fostering parents; these adoption orders will be made on direct application to the relevant court. If a young person is in the care of the local authority the natural parents will be asked to give their consent to the adoption, because of the finality of the step.

Being adopted through an agency or the social services

Adoption agencies draw up strict guidelines when they are selecting adoptive parents. For example:

1. All adoptive parents must be at least 21 years old.
2. Depending on the age and the health of the young person concerned, the agency may allow both single people and couples, married and unmarried, to adopt. Divorced people who have remarried may also be allowed to adopt.
3. Families with children will also be considered.
4. There are no restrictions about the level of income of adoptive parents, although an agency would want to know how things would be arranged if both parents were working.
5. There is no legal requirement to make sure that young people are adopted by adults of their own race, but some adoption agencies have made this a matter of policy for social and religious reasons.

The adoption agency will spend a long time finding out about the prospective adoptive parents. There will have been several meetings between the parents and the agency before they are accepted and introduced to a young person who is available for adoption. They will have had a medical examination, and several interviews, together and separately if there are two of them. There will also have been a check to see if they have any history of mental illness or a criminal record. So, if you are in care, anyone who expresses an interest in adopting you will have been very carefully screened before they have been allowed to meet you.

In order to make sure that an adoption is satisfactory from everyone's point of view the adoption agency will also know a lot about you, the young person to be adopted. They will know:

1. All about your background, including any health problems.
2. Why your natural parents decided to have you adopted.
3. Whether your natural parents ask that you be placed with a family of a particular faith.

If you have strong feelings about who you are adopted by, then make sure that the adoption agency or social services know. You can do this by speaking to your social worker or anyone employed by the social services department.

If particular adults decide that they would like to adopt you, a number of meetings and visits will be arranged, some with a social worker present, some where you will be alone with your prospective parents. If there are already children in the family you will be given a chance to get to know them and you will also visit the family at home. These visits will go on until everyone – you, your adoptive parents and the agency – are sure that the time has come for you to go and live with them.

An adoption does not become final because you have agreed to go and live with your adoptive parents. A court will not formalise any order until a probationary period has passed – at least three months. During this time your natural parents or the social services retain all parental rights. Your natural parents still have the right to change their minds about the adoption, even if the social services have all parental rights over you. But if the social services consider that your natural parents are behaving unreasonably they can apply to the court to ask that the need for your natural parents' permission be dispensed with. This request to the court may also be made if your parents have abandoned or neglected you, or failed to fulfil their parental obligations towards you.

During the probationary period you will be visited by various people from the social services, the adoption agency and possibly a court welfare officer.

Applying for a formal adoption order

If the probationary period is a success your prospective parents formally apply to adopt you. This application will be made to either the magistrates court or to the county court. The adoption agency or social services department will advise your prospective parents about the correct procedure, and you will have to attend court on the day that the adoption order is heard.

After an adoption order is made

Once an adoption order has been made:

1. A copy of the adoption order will be made in the Adoption Register, to replace the original birth certificate. When you are 18 you have the opportunity to trace your natural parents.
2. You will no longer have any contact with your natural parents, unless your adoptive parents have previously agreed to this or the court has ordered it, but this is exceptional.
3. The formal visits from social workers will cease, although many social services departments and adoption agencies provide post-adoption support and advice.

Adoption by a step-parent

As we have already seen, merely marrying one of your parents does not give your step-parent parental rights. Many couples who marry after one of them (or both) has previously been divorced decide that it would be the best thing for the new parents to adopt all the children in the family. However, a court will not necessarily agree to this. Adoption, as we have said, takes away all the rights of the natural parent and the court often prefers the children to stay in touch with both their natural parents following a divorce. Instead, the new parents may have to consider guardianship or formalising their intention by expressing their wishes in their wills.

If your parent and step-parent decide that they want to adopt you, they have to apply to the county court for permission and also advise the local social services department of their intention to adopt. They may feel at this stage that they would like to consult a solicitor. Your local Citizen's Advice Bureau will advise you of the local solicitors who specialise in family and child care law.

The procedure is similar to that of the adoption as described above, except of course that there will be no period of introduction. There will, however, be a period of visits by social workers, etc. The court will only make its decision when it has considered all the circumstances of the case. This will mean looking at all the reports, and taking into account both your wishes and the wishes of your natural parent. And in the end the court may decide that it will not allow your step-parent to adopt you because it wishes you to retain contact with your natural parents.

Relatives and foster parents wishing to adopt

Relatives wishing to adopt children will follow the same procedure as step-parents, unless the young person is in the care of the local authority, when they will be required to follow the same route as any other prospective parent wishing to adopt.

Foster parents will apply to the county court and inform the local social services of their intention to adopt. If they are fostering on behalf of the local authority, their application will not be considered until they have fostered the particular young person for at least five years. Private foster parents can apply to adopt after a year.

FOSTERING

Foster parents provide a home for young people in care. There are different types of foster parent. Some look after children and young people for short periods, until they return to their parents. Or they may foster a child to provide a breathing space for a family during a crisis, or while the social services department make decisions about a young person's long-term future. Or they may provide a permanent home for someone.

Although foster parents have the day-to-day responsibility for looking after a child or young person, they never have full parental rights – they can only acquire these through adoption (see above).

CARE

There are different reasons why young people go into care.
They may be placed there by their parents who, for
various reasons are unable to look after them. Or a baby
may have been abandoned, or both its parents have died.
This is known as **voluntary care** or being looked after
by the authority. Parents then have a right to have their
children back at home, providing they give the social
services notice and proceedings have not begun or
parental responsibility has not passed to the local social
services department. This sometimes happens, and
because of this parents are sometimes reluctant to put
their children into voluntary care.

Responsibilities of the local authority social services department

If a child or young person is taken into care, the local
authority, through the social services department, takes
on the parental responsibility for them. As well as being
responsible for the young person they have certain duties.

1. They must regularly **review** any order that has been
    made, to see that it is being carried out effectively.
2. **Access** – if a child or young person has been placed in
    a children's home or with foster parents the social
    services must encourage the parents to see the child,
    unless a court forbids this.
3. **Independent visitors** – if a child or young person
    has not had a visit from their parents for over a year
    an independent visitor should be appointed. These are
    normally social workers not employed by the local
    authority that has responsibility for the young person.
4. If a child or young person is likely to suffer harm
    then there must be provision for **secure
    accommodation**.
5. The social services department must have developed
    arrangements to prepare a young person for **leaving
    care** when they are 18 or 19.

WHEN THINGS GO WRONG IN THE FAMILY

6. **Complaints** – children, parents and foster parents
   must have the opportunity to complain to an
   independent body. However the social services
   department is not bound by any decisions taken.

Why might you be taken into care

You might be taken into care because the social services
department decides that your parents cannot or should
not be allowed to look after you. This maybe because you
have been, or it is suspected that you may have been,
physically or sexually abused by a member of your family.
This can be done under an **emergency order**, provided
a court is satisfied that there is reasonable cause to do so.
An emergency order can last for up to eight days, and can
be extended for another seven days if a court can be
convinced that this would be appropriate. The court will
assume that the social services will allow you to have
contact with your family and that any necessary medical
checks will take place. After this emergency order has
been operating for 72 hours, then either you or your
parents or whoever looks after you have the right to ask
for the order to cease.

It may be that there are other stresses in your family.
You or one of your brothers or sisters may be severely
disabled and your parents no longer able to provide you all
with the necessary care. Or you may be housed in very
bad conditions or your family feel that you are beyond
their control or you may have committed a serious
criminal offence. The social services department will have
to convince a court that in one of these situations you are
at risk or may suffer and come to some harm.

Being in care or under a supervision order does not
always mean that you will be taken away from your
parents.

What happens when you go to court

Applications for care orders are heard in the juvenile
court. If a child is under five years old they do not have to
attend the court hearing, but once you are five you are

expected to be present for at least part of the proceedings.
The court will not expect you to speak for yourself but will
appoint an adult to help you, a **guardian ad litem**, one
of a number of people who are members of a local panel of
guardians. They will probably be trained as social workers
but they are totally independent, not employed by social
services. Once appointed it is their responsibility to see
that your interests are looked after and that your point of
view is put to the court. There is no defined age limit to
say whether or not your opinion is put forward. It all
depends on your particular circumstances, such as
physical or mental handicap.

Together you and your guardian *ad litem* may decide
that you should have a solicitor to represent you in court.
You should not have to pay as the costs will be met by the
Legal Aid Fund. If you have a guardian *ad litem* who does
not think you need a solicitor but you do, then you can ask
the court to appoint you one; you have the right to see this
solicitor on your own without your guardian *ad litem* being
present.

The court hearing
When the day of the hearing arrives you will find that
there are a lot of people in the court room.

1. There will be two or three magistrates who have had
    special training, sitting at a table or at a raised desk.
2. There will be a court clerk.
3. There will be you, your guardian *ad litem* and your
    solicitor.
4. There will be the social worker representing the social
    services department who are applying for the care or
    supervision order, and a social services department
    solicitor.
5. Your parents may also be present with their solicitor.
    If your parents are separated and in dispute then they
    may each bring a solicitor.

Before making a decision the magistrates will hear the

social services' arguments as to why you should be taken into care. Then your parents, through their solicitors, can put their points of view. You will also have your say. Any reports that have been prepared about the circumstances of the case will be presented to the court and the solicitors will be able to raise queries if any of the information is inaccurate. You should let your solicitor know if anything is wrong in the reports.

When the magistrates have heard all the opinions and reports then they will make a decision. They may decide to make a **care order**, in which case the social services will take responsibility for you. The social services may then decide that:

1. You are to be taken away from your parents and never see them again.
2. You are taken away from your parents and then, after a time of planned meetings and visits, you may eventually go back to live with your parents.

The court may decide to grant a **supervision order**, and then the social services may decide that:

3. You stay at home but be closely supervised by a social worker. This arrangement will involve visits from the social worker who will try to involve you in activities outside the home.
4. You go to live with one of your parents and both your parents and a social worker will work out a plan of visits to your other parent.

If you are 17 you cannot be taken into voluntary care, even if it has been requested. However, you can be committed to care by a court order when you are 17 and remain there until you are 19.

If a care or supervision order is made because you have suffered violence from one of your parents then your solicitor should make a claim for compensation on your behalf to the Criminal Injuries Compensation Board.

What should you expect while you are living in care?

If you are taken away from your parents you will probably
live in a **community home** or with a **foster family**.
Later you may live with foster parents (see Fostering,
page 41). It may be that eventually the social services try
to find you a permanent home with either long-term foster
parents, or put you up for adoption (see Adoption, page
35), but this will only happen if you **agree**, and you will
be prepared for this if the time comes.

The community home will be staffed by social workers.
Often you will live in a small house group, and you may
have to share a bedroom. You should be given pocket
money and a clothing allowance. If you are still living in
care when you start work you will have to contribute from
your own earnings, exactly as you would do if you were
living at home.

If you don't get on with your particular social worker,
you can always ask to change. Be prepared to speak to a
senior social worker if you are unhappy. If a number of
things are wrong write them down so that when you are
interviewed you will remember everything that you want
to say. (See Useful addresses for the names of
organisations that can help you if you have a problem
while you are living in care.)

While you are in care the social services take on all the
parental responsibility for you, but this does not mean
that you do not have any rights. You have the same right
to education, medical and dental treatment, contraceptive
advice, employment, to get married, to practise your
religion, as any other young person. Even if you share a
room you should have the right to some privacy and space
to keep your personal possessions.

If the need arises to punish you then the punishments
should be the same as if you were at home – stopping of
pocket money, restrictions on going out, etc. Corporal
punishment is not allowed in local authority homes, nor
should you be locked in a room on your own. If this
happens you should complain.

Many social services departments encourage all the young people in their care to keep a personal record of themselves, which they keep all the time they stay in care. It can contain information about themselves, where they were born, their natural family including brothers and sisters, where they lived, their foster parents, their schools, etc.

If your parents do not or are prevented from seeing you then you have the right to have an independent visitor see you regularly. They will not be a social services' employee and should be there to look after your interests if you are in any conflict with your social worker.

What you should expect when you leave care
Once a care or supervision order is made it does not have to stay in force until you are 18. For example, it may be part of the social services' arrangements that you regularly visit your parents and then stay maybe for a night or a weekend visit. After a while it may be agreed that it is all right for you to live at home; then the social services department will ask to have the care order **revoked**, i.e. finished.

Once you are 16 you can begin to discuss leaving care anyway, providing you can convince your social worker that you can look after yourself, support yourself financially and find somewhere to live. But this is not easy. (See Chapter 7, When you decide to leave home.) Your social worker may arrange for you to live in a hostel, or they may sponsor an application to be housed by the local council. You may have to do this anyway if you want to continue your education and the college or school is far away from where you are at present living.

If everyone, especially you, agrees that it is a good idea for you to leave care then the court generally agrees and cancels the care order. If you want to leave and are satisfied that you can look after yourself but the social worker does not agree, then you have the right to go to court, with a solicitor to argue your case. The court will then decide what is in your best interests.

4. WHEN YOU WANT TO GET A JOB

When I started my Saturday job six months ago, I really enjoyed it. Three weeks ago my employers sold their cafe and new people took over. I used to do waitressing but now they're asking me to wash the floors and clean out the kitchen when the cook has gone home. They are saying that I can't have my lunch break as that is when we are very busy, but I can have half an hour in the afternoon when we're quieter. I'm 15 and I need the money as I'm saving up for a holiday. Can they make me do all this work?

IF YOU ARE UNDER 13

No one under the age of 13 may be employed. You may carry out an errand for a friend or neighbour, but they should not pay you. The only exception to this is where you are employed by a member of your family. In some areas (inner London, for example) you can work for your parents or guardians in light horticultural work once you are 12.

BETWEEN 13 AND 16

If you are between 13 and 16 you may get a job, but you will find that there are local byelaws as well as statutes (Acts of Parliament) to restrict what you are allowed to do. You are also restricted in the number of hours that you are allowed to work.

Hours

1. You cannot work before 7 o'clock in the morning or after 7 in the evening on any day.
2. You are not allowed to work for more than two hours on any school day.
3. You may not work for more than two hours on a Sunday.
4. You should not do a job if it involves you carrying, lifting or moving anything that might injure you.

Local byelaws may further restrict what you can do; for example, in Norwich you may not be allowed to work at all on a Sunday.

When you are 15 you can work for eight hours a day on Saturday or during the school holidays, but even in the holidays you can't work more than 20 hours a week if you are under 15, or 30 hours when you are over 15.

Where you may not work

Several laws stop you working in certain jobs. You cannot work in a mine, or in a docks or sewage works. You cannot sell or collect scrap metal or work as a window cleaner. Again local byelaws differ; you can always check with your local education office or Citizen's Advice Bureau.

Employment cards

Local authorities will issue employment cards or permits to young people between the ages of 13 and 16, and most reputable employers will not employ young people without one.

The employer will be required to notify the local authority of your name, address, date of birth, where you will be employed, what you will be doing and what hours you will be working. The local authority will then issue an employment card or permit which you will be required to produce if requested.

ONCE YOU ARE 16

Even though you may have left school, there will still be
regulations governing what hours you are allowed to work
and what you can do. If you are still at school and working
in the evenings or at the weekend then the same rules
apply.

Hours and meals breaks

1. You cannot work for more than 48 hours in any week,
   although if you work in a shop that serves meals or
   refreshments you can work for up to 48 hours a week.
2. You are allowed to do occasional overtime, but this
   must not be for more than six hours in any one week or
   for more than a total of 50 hours in any year or in a
   period of more than 12 weeks.
3. If you work for more than five hours then you must
   have a break of 30 minutes, either to eat or just to rest.
4. If you are working between the hours of 11.30 am and
   2.30 pm you should have a dinner break of 45 minutes
   within these times.
5. If you work on a Sunday you must be given a day off
   in lieu – in its place – either in the week before the
   Sunday you work or in the week immediately after the
   Sunday you have worked.
6. At least one day in your working week you should
   finish work by 1 pm.

The 1988 Employment Act will, unless it is amended,
remove many of the restrictions placed on the hours that
young people are allowed to work. For example 16–18 year
olds will be able to work for more than 48 hours a week in
shops and factories, and will also be allowed to work night
shifts. While restrictions on working with dangerous
machinery and substances will remain, there will no
longer be any guaranteed meal breaks.

Where you may not work
You are not allowed to work in a bar or any other place licensed to sell alcohol during opening hours, including off licences. You may not work in a betting shop.

Employers' responsibilities
Any employer of young people is obliged to keep records of the hours they work, when they take their breaks, how much overtime they have worked, and must put up a notice setting out all the working conditions.

Health and safety
All employees, not just young people, are protected by rules concerning health and safety at work. Government inspectors enforce these rules, which cover guards on machinery, rubbish in the workplace, working with dangerous substances and procedures for dealing with accidents. They also will check to see that there are the right number of toilets and washbasins for employees, whether or not there are adequate fire precautions, and that all employees know what to do if there is a fire.

If you feel that your employers are not conforming to the regulations, then you can either talk to your local trades union representative, if you have one, or inform the health and safety officer yourself (you will find the phone number under Health and Safety Executive). Your call will be treated in confidence and the health and safety officer can make a spot check to assess the situation.

IF YOU WORK ILLEGALLY
In the past few years there has been concern expressed that many young children are working illegally. A survey by the Low Pay Unit in 1983 showed that a very large number of under 16s who were working were doing so illegally, generally in occupations that were forbidden to them, such as heavy manual work or for far longer hours than was permitted. As we have seen, the rules and regulations covering the employment of young people are varied and complex and because the responsibility of

enforcing them is spread between many different agencies, e.g. local council, local education office, they are often difficult to enforce.

If your school finds out you are working illegally your teacher or school counsellor may try and persuade you to give up your job. They will also talk to your parents about it. The power to prosecute employers lies with the education welfare office. They have limited powers to question employers and any prosecution would order you to give up your job on the grounds that it is bad for your health and your education. The problem is that education welfare officers have no power to enter the workplace and examine what goes on there. As checking on illegal work practices is only part of their job, very few prosecutions are brought each year.

Many parents find it difficult to stop their children working as the extra money forms a necessary addition to the family budget. The most likely way illegal working will be discovered is during a random inspection by either the environmental health officer or the health and safety inspector.

FINDING A JOB

While you are still at school you will probably have discussions, either as a group or individually, with your careers officer. Local firms may offer the chance to look around their factory or office while you are still at school and will probably come along to a careers convention or evening to show you what openings they have for young people, or you may have the opportunity to take part in a work experience programme during school time.

However, if you leave school or college without making a decision then you should go to your local careers office to see what they can offer. Don't assume that they are going to send you on to the Youth Training Scheme. (You will find the careers office listed under Careers advice in the Yellow Pages.) Other places to look for jobs locally are the Jobcentre, situations vacant columns in the paper,

WHEN YOU WANT TO GET A JOB

situations vacant boards outside local factories, or adverts
in shop windows. You could try employment agencies, but
they tend to specialise in finding jobs for people with
particular skills, so when you are first looking for work
they may not be appropriate.

APPLYING FOR A JOB

Once you have seen a job, the next step is formally
applying. Some adverts tell you to send for an application
form, some will ask for a handwritten letter, while others
ask for a cv. It is important to do what is asked of you.

Curriculum vitae

It will always be useful to have a summary of details
about yourself. This is where your cv or curriculum vitae
comes in handy. Even if the job application doesn't ask
for one it is helpful for reference. A curriculum vitae
should contain details of:

1. Name, address and telephone number.
2. Date of birth and current age.
3. Schools attended – names, addresses and dates.
4. Colleges attended – names, addresses and dates.
5. Qualifications (if any) – names of exams, subject,
    grades.
6. Previous employment – including Saturday and
    holiday jobs.
7. Voluntary work – community activities, fund raising.
8. Hobbies and interests – you may want to put them all
    down, or just put in the ones that fit a particular job.
9. Education and training at present – this can include
    evening classes or any course that you are taking.
10. Referees – the names and addresses of at least two
    people who know you, such as teachers, youth
    workers, past employers, or just neighbours.

Try to get your cv typed if you can, and take several good
photocopies.

If you are sent an application form to be completed, but all it asks is for information that is on your cv don't be tempted to send them a cv and the incomplete form. Fill the form in using your cv information.

If you are asked to write a personal letter, it probably means that the employer is interested in getting someone who is capable of writing clearly and expressing themselves in their own words. Again use the information you have, don't send in the typed cv.

Attending an interview

Good preparation will help you through an interview.

1. Find out where the interview is being held and the best way to get there. This will ensure that you arrive on time.
2. Get a good night's sleep the night before.
3. Dress so that you look smart and feel comfortable. Make sure they remember you for your abilities, not the scruffy or outrageous clothes.
4. When you get into the interview sit down when you are asked. Try to remember the interviewer's name, and use it. Look at them when you speak, and speak clearly. Watch carefully as you give your answers so that you don't go on too long answering one question. However, the interviewer is trying to find out about you, so if you think you have experience which is appropriate try and get that across.
5. Prospective employers will expect to be asked questions about the job and the company; it shows that you are interested in that particular job, not just in any job.
6. If you are offered the job, don't be afraid to ask about hours, rates of pay and how you will be paid, holidays, overtime and possibilities for further training.

DISCRIMINATION IN SELECTION FOR JOBS AND AT WORK

Two pieces of legislation, the Race Relations Act and Sex Discrimination Act, make it an offence for an employer, trade union or employment agency to discriminate against you because of your race, sex or colour. This applies to recruitment as well as when you are at work. The difficulty with these laws is proving that such discrimination has taken place. Your employer does not have to tell you why you have been turned down for a job.

If you feel that you have been discriminated against when being interviewed for a job, discuss the problem either with your local community relations council, Citizen's Advice Bureau or law centre to see if it is worth pursuing a claim.

WHEN YOU GET A JOB HOW DOES THE LAW PROTECT YOU?

Employment law gives all employees certain basic rights. Very often certain employers will offer better terms and conditions of employment than the law requires, but they cannot offer you worse conditions.

When you first start, you will possibly find it unsettling. For one thing you may have to get up earlier, you may work longer without a break, and after initial training you may work unsupervised. In the first few weeks you are bound to be very tired at the end of the day, but at least when you finish work your time is your own.

If you think it is taking you too long to settle, try talking to other new employees to see how they are getting on. Larger firms have a personnel manager whose job it is to look after employees, particularly new ones.

Payment

One of the questions that you should ask at your interview is 'How will I be paid? Will it be weekly, fortnightly or monthly? In cash, or do I need to open a bank account?

Nowadays because of the difficulties of handling large amounts of cash many employers prefer to pay wages and salaries into bank accounts. (See Opening a bank account, page 107.) Regardless of how your money is paid, every payday you should receive a payslip showing what you have earned and what deductions for tax and national insurance have been made. An itemised pay statement is a legal right.

Terms and conditions

If you are working more than 16 hours a week, within 13 weeks of starting work you should receive a written statement of your terms and conditions of employment. If you work 8 hours but less than 16 hours a week you are entitled to the same after 5 years. The statement must include:

1. Your name and your employer's name.
2. Title of job and place of work.
3. Date employment started.
4. Expiry date of contract if it's for a fixed term.
5. Hours of work.
6. Holidays and holiday pay.
7. Sick pay, if any.
8. Pension scheme.
9. Length of notice.
10. Trade union rights.
11. Grievance procedure.
12. Disciplinary procedure.

You may be asked to sign a copy of this statement. It is not in itself your contract of employment, but by signing it you are accepting it as a complete statement of the terms of your contract of employment.

Other rights

1. You have the right to belong to a trade union.
2. If you become pregnant your employer should allow

you paid time off to attend antenatal classes, and if you have worked for at least 16 hours a week for 2 years with the same employer you have the right to return to work after the baby is born.

3. The right to equal pay means that men and women have the right to be paid the same wages for doing the same or broadly similar work.

4. You have the right to statutory sick pay (SSP) if you are sick for more than four days. Unless you have an agreement with your employer to make up your wages or to pay you for the first three days of sickness, you will receive nothing except SSP at a flat rate. SSP is paid for 28 weeks in any one year.

5. If you have an accident at work you should report it straight away, either to your foreman or someone senior. You should try and make sure that it is entered in the company's accident book. If you are going to be sick because of your injury, then as well as claiming SSP you should also make a claim for industrial injury benefit. Your local Citizen's Advice Bureau can tell you how to claim.

WHAT HAPPENS IF YOU LOSE YOUR JOB?

If you are unfortunate enough to lose your job, always check that the correct dismissal procedure has been followed. Unless you are dismissed for gross misconduct, you have the right to notice and any holiday money that is due to you. If you have worked for more than four weeks you are entitled to one week's notice, then one week for every complete year of service, up to a maximum of 12 weeks. If you wish to give notice, the same rules apply, unless your terms and conditions of employment state otherwise. Always try to give the proper notice, even if you have another job to go to. You may be penalised if you don't, if for example the new job fails to materialise and you have to sign on at the unemployment benefit office.

If your employer dismisses you for gross misconduct then you forfeit many of these rights. Gross misconduct means that your employer has reason to believe that you have been stealing, for example. If you feel that he has behaved unreasonably you should contact your local law centre or Citizen's Advice Bureau. You cannot ask for your claim for unfair dismissal to be heard by an industrial tribunal until you have been employed for two years if you work full time, and five years if you work less than 16 hours a week.

Your employer may make you redundant, because he no longer has enough work for you. You cannot be penalised by the unemployment benefit office if you lose your job in this way. However, you will not be able to claim a redundancy payment until you have been employed for two years, and service under the age of 18 does not count.

If you have been employed for more than 16 hours a week and you have worked for longer than six months (two years under 1988 Employment Act), then you are entitled to receive a statement from your employer giving the reasons for your dismissal. If you work for less than 16 hours a week you need to have been employed for five years.

What should you do if you lose your job?

Your employer should give you your P45 when you leave his employment, as well as any wages that he might owe you. You should inform the unemployment benefit office that you are no longer employed and wish to claim benefit. As you are under 18 you will not have enough contributions to get unemployment benefit, but you may be able to get income support – check Chapter 7 to see if you will be eligible. If you lost your job through gross misconduct or you were dismissed, any income support you receive will be reduced while investigations are made.

If you lose your part-time job while you are still at school

If you are dismissed from your part-time job and you think this was unreasonable, particularly if you were sacked because you refused to do a dangerous job or refused to work too many hours, then you should report the matter to the educational welfare officer. It won't guarantee that you will get your job back, but it might help prevent other young people being exploited.

WHY NATIONAL INSURANCE AND INCOME TAX ARE DEDUCTED

National insurance
A national insurance number is issued by the DSS so that a record can be kept of all national insurance contributions paid throughout your working life. You should receive a plastic card showing your national insurance number around the time of your 16th birthday. If it doesn't arrive contact your local DSS office. A national insurance number consists of two letters, six numbers and one letter, for example BS 985672 Y.

If you are employed you will pay class 1 national insurance contributions once your weekly earnings go above the lower earnings limit (1989–90 £43 a week). Your employer also makes a contribution. National insurance contributions count towards a number of benefits, e.g. retirement pension, sickness benefit, unemployment benefit. However there are always other conditions attached to receiving these benefits, apart from just having paid contributions.

If you stay at school after you are 16 you will be given starter credits to help you when you do start work.

Income tax
Once you are born you can be liable for income tax, but most people only begin to pay when they start work. An income tax allowance will be allocated to you by the tax office, who will tell your employer. He will then deduct the tax from your wages, and send it to the Inland Revenue.

Your tax allowance depends upon your individual circumstances, but unless you are married or have children you will be given the single person's tax allowance (1989–90 £2785). This means that once you earn more than this in any tax year (beginning of April–end of March) your employer will deduct tax. But you will find that deductions are averaged out over a whole year, so that you don't have to pay a lot all at once. At the end of each tax year you will be sent a tax return so that the Inland Revenue can check that you are paying the correct amount of tax. You are responsible for completing and returning this form. It will ask you how much you have earned in the previous year. Your employer should provide you with a P60 form which will give you all this information.

If you change jobs during a tax year, your employer should give you a P45 to take to your new employer. This will tell your new employer how much tax and national insurance you have paid in the correct tax year, and your current tax code. This means that your new employer will be able to deduct tax from your pay at the correct rate rather than using an emergency code which means that tax would be taken from you at a much higher rate.

OTHER TYPES OF EMPLOYMENT AND TRAINING SCHEMES

Apprenticeships

Apprenticeships are a specialised form of training, over a considerable number of years. They have traditionally been found in male dominated areas of work such as building and engineering, but a notable exception to this is hairdressing. Because under-18s are held not to be able to make contracts, your parents would sign an apprenticeship agreement on your behalf. The contract is binding and gives details of hours, wages, and length of training.

An apprenticeship cannot guarantee you a job at the end of your training nor can it prevent you being dismissed. If your employer dismisses you from your apprenticeship before the completion of the agreed term then all the rules of notice as shown above apply, but he does not have to give you notice at the end of your apprenticeship.

Armed forces

A boy is allowed to join the forces when he is 16; a girl must wait until she is 17. Both require their parents' permission if they are under 18. Local recruitment offices can be found by looking under Army, Navy and Royal Air Force in the phone book.

Youth Training Scheme

The Youth Training Scheme (YTS) guarantees every 16-year-old school leaver a two-year work experience and training programme; if you leave school at 17 you can join a one-year course. Details of both schemes and their local availability can be obtained through your careers office. Try to choose a scheme which offers you the most in the way of opportunities and training.

You will be paid a weekly allowance and, if it is appropriate, travel and accommodation allowances. It may also be possible for you to claim housing benefit (see Chapter 7). If you have just left school your parents may continue to receive child benefit for you, for up to 12 weeks. If you are still waiting for a YTS place after this time you may receive a bridging allowance, which can be paid for eight weeks in any 12-month period.

When you are allocated a YTS place you should be given a training agreement which contains information about the placement – the hours of work, what happens when you are sick, holiday entitlement, time off for interviews, disciplinary procedures. While on YTS you have the right to belong to a trade union.

Your placing should be a mixture of work experience and training, perhaps leading to a recognised qualification. If you feel that this is not what you are getting and you are unable to get any satisfaction from your managing agent – the official responsible for you while on YTS – you may want to discuss the problem with the careers office. It may be that you are entitled to leave the scheme you are on and be transferred to another scheme. If, however, you are dismissed the rights to notice do not apply, nor can you get written reasons for your dismissal.

At the end of the scheme, you are not guaranteed a job, so you may have to sign on and claim income support (see Chapter 7).

5. WHEN YOU WANT TO TRAVEL

I want to go on holiday abroad this summer with some friends from college. I've discovered that I need a full passport. My parents don't like the idea of my going away and they are saying that they won't let me get a passport. Can they do this? I'm 17 next month.

IN THE UNITED KINGDOM

Bus and Underground

Once you are five years old you will have to pay a child's fare, usually half the adult fare, on a bus. This will also apply on the London Underground. On the Glasgow Underground, you pay the adult rate at 16. The Newcastle Metro charges a child rate of 10 pence for anyone under the age of 14. In some parts of the country if there is more than one child under five travelling with an adult and one child takes up a seat, then the parent will have to pay a child's fare for them as well.

Once you are over 14 years of age you have to pay full fare on buses in most parts of the country, although in London you wait until you are 16. However, most bus companies offer discounts and student tickets to encourage you to travel by bus – go to your nearest bus station and ask. It may be that when you are choosing a secondary school at 12+, the cost of getting there is an important consideration; see Chapter 2, page 17, to see if you would qualify for free transport.

If you travel by coach your local bus or coach station will know about a student coach card. It costs £3.90 a year (1989) and can be used to get discounts on National Express buses.

Trains

Your parents will have to pay a child's fare once you are five and full fares when you reach 16. However, British Rail offer so many types of special tickets and discounts that you rarely have to pay the normal fare.

1. British Rail Rail Riders, their young rail users club, give free travel vouchers when you join.
2. With a Family Rail Card adults and children get reduced fares. Children under the age of 16 travel for £1 if they travel with a card carrying adult.
3. Once you are 16 you can apply for a Young Person's Rail Card. At present (1989) this costs £15 a year, providing you are still in full-time education or studying at a college for over 15 hours a week for 20 weeks in a year. This rail card gives you at least one-third off most fares, and also gives you access to European rail travel.
4. Network South East offer a Network Card for just £5 to Student Rail Card holders, for use in their area.
5. If you do get the chance to go abroad, British Rail have an Inter Rail card for people under the age of 26. This card gives you one month's travel in most of Europe and Scandinavia for £146 (1989).

If you enjoy cycling, British Rail publishes a *Guide to Biking by Train,* which tells you which trains you can use and the reservation charges made for bicycles.

Information about all these is available at any British rail station.

DRIVING

Forms for all vehicle licences are available from main post offices.

Bicycle

You should not ride a bicycle on the road until you have had some training. If you cause an accident you may be sued by another driver and treated just like any other driver who commits a motoring offence (see Negligence, page 4). If you ride on the footpath you could be committing an offence. Most LEAs, in conjunction with the Royal Society for the Prevention of Accidents (RoSPA) or the local police force, run training courses.

Motor cycle

You can apply for a provisional licence to drive a motor cycle when you are 17. You cannot ride a motor cycle with an engine bigger than 125cc and you must take both parts of the motor cycle test within two years of getting your provisional licence. You can no longer drive indefinitely on a provisional licence.

Moped

You can apply for a provisional licence to ride a moped when you are 16, but you cannot ride a moped with an engine bigger than 50 cc and it cannot go faster than 30 mph. However, you can continue to ride a moped with a provisional licence for as long as you like.

Motor car

You can apply for a provisional licence to drive a motor car when you are 17, but until you have passed your test you must have a qualified driver with you.

Glider, plane or helicopter

When you are 17 you can apply to become a pilot in charge of a glider. You can also take flying lessons and train to become a pilot or a helicopter pilot.

PASSPORTS

If you are under 18 you will need your parents consent if you want to apply for a passport; the only exceptions are if you are serving in the armed forces or if you are married.

If your parents are married only one has to give permission; if they are divorced only one parent has to

agree, unless the arrangements that the court have made
for your care at the time of the divorce say that both
parents have to make joint decisions. This is often done to
prevent one parent from taking a child out of the country
without the other parent's permission. If you are in care,
the local authority will have to give its consent, and if you
are in voluntary care then your parents will also have to
give permission.

Until you are 16 you can be included on one of your
parent's passports. This means that you can only travel
abroad with that parent. If you go away with a school
party the school will apply for a collective passport. If you
are under 16 and you need a passport separate from that
of your parents then you can have a standard passport
lasting for five years, which can be extended for another
five years if necessary. It costs £15 and you apply on
passport form B.

British visitors passport

If you are going to certain countries, you can apply for a
British visitors passport once you are eight years old. This
costs £7.50 and you get it from main post offices on any
weekday except Saturday. You will need two photographs
of yourself, two means of identification, for example a
birth certificate, a National Savings book or a medical
card. You must be present when it is issued, and your
parents will still have to sign the form. These passports
last for one year only. You can use a British visitors
passport if you wish to visit most European and
Scandinavian countries; a full list is given on the
application form.

Standard passport

Once you are 16 years old you can apply for a standard
passport. You apply on passport form A, and you will
need a fee of £15 and two photographs signed by someone
like a doctor, a magistrate, a minister or priest who has
known you for at least two years, and some means of
identification such as a birth certificate. You can get the

form from a main post office, but you send it to the nearest passport office, the address of which will be on the form. It takes about four weeks to issue a passport, sometimes longer in the summer, so if you have a particular date for travelling make sure that you send in the application forms in good time. In an emergency you should tell the passport office and send some sort of evidence why you need the passport urgently, to speed things up.

IMMIGRATION RULES

Anyone born in the United Kingdom before 1 January 1983 is a British citizen. This means that they can live and work in the UK without any restriction.

If you weren't born here then you will probably have the same immigration status as your parents. If you or your parents are not sure what your immigration status is then take your passport to the nearest Citizen's Advice Bureau and they will try to work it out for you. The stamps put into passports by immigration officers can tell you a great deal about your rights while you are living in the UK.

Your citizenship or status can also depend on whether or not your parents are married. If your parents are not married and in the eyes of the law you are illegitimate, then your status relies on that of your mother, not your father. Since 1 January 1983 a child born in the UK whose parents are not married will only be entitled to British citizenship if their mother is a British citizen or is settled here. So if your mother is not British and your father is, but they are not married, then you cannot have British citizenship.

However, if you have lived in the UK for 10 years without being out of the country for 90 days in any one year, you can still contact the Home Office to see if they will grant you citizenship. The Home office has discretionary powers to grant certain groups of people citizenship, such as refugees or stateless persons.

6.
WHEN YOU GET INTO TROUBLE

Last week when my friends and I were walking home from the pictures, a policemen stopped us and started to ask questions. He then asked one of my friends to take off his anorak. Then he looked into the pockets. After a few more questions he told us all 'Get off home.' Some of us were very frightened, some were crying. Did the policeman have the right to do this or should he have asked our parents for permission? We are all 14 and 15 years old.

How you are treated by the courts if you are found guilty of an offence depends on your age.

1. If you are under 10 years old you cannot be found guilty of an offence. But if you are under 10 and have committed a criminal offence, care proceedings may be started by the local social services (see Chapter 3).
2. If you are between 10 and 14 years old, you can only be convicted of an offence if the prosecution proves not only that you actually committed the offence itself but that you knew what you were doing was seriously wrong.
3. If you are between 10 and 17 years old you will be dealt with by the juvenile court.
4. Young people aged 17 but under 21 are dealt with by the adult courts in the same way as older people, except that they cannot be sentenced to imprisonment, and can only be given custodial sentences in very limited circumstances.

CONTACT WITH THE POLICE

Stopped by a policeman in the street

A policeman is allowed to stop anyone and ask them questions to find out if they have committed or intend to commit a crime. If a policeman has reason to suspect that you are carrying stolen or what are called prohibited articles he can search you or the vehicle in which you are travelling, and ask you questions (prohibited articles can be anything that could be used or adapted for use as an offensive weapon or to commit a burglary, theft, stealing a car, etc.) A policeman must have grounds – good reasons – if he wants to search you. If there are no grounds then they can still watch you or ask you questions. In some parts of the country the police seem to find the behaviour of young people suspect, and often stop and search them in the street or while they are driving a vehicle, for no apparent reason. Therefore it is to your advantage to know how to behave if you are stopped and what the police should or should not do.

The police are not allowed to argue that their reasonable suspicions for stopping and searching you are based on your colour, being out in a group, previous offences, dress or hairstyle.

If you are stopped by a policeman you are entitled to expect that they will tell you their name, or show you a warrant card if they are in plain clothes, and tell you which police station they are attached to. They should also explain the grounds for their wish to search you and what they expect to find. If the police do carry out a search then they are required to complete a record of the search, and you have a right to a copy of this report within the following 12 months.

A search carried out in public is restricted. A police officer is only allowed to ask you to remove your coat, jacket and gloves, shoes and hat, but you can volunteer to have other items of clothing searched. If the search is conducted in a police station or in a police van or at home you can be searched more thoroughly. If you are searched thoroughly you can expect it to be carried out by an officer of the same sex as yourself.

When you are stopped and perhaps searched by the police in public, it is very difficult to know how to react. The whole procedure is embarrassing and you may feel humiliated in front of your friends. But you should try and keep as calm as possible; it helps you to concentrate and doesn't allow the situation to deteriorate to the point where the police carry out a search or an arrest that they hadn't originally intended, simply because they feel that you are acting suspiciously. For example, if you refuse to be searched, the police have the right to use reasonable force. Being calm also helps you subsequently to remember what you said, which may be important if you end up going to the police station or, in extreme circumstances, want to complain.

BEING ARRESTED

Young people are usually arrested in the following situations:

1. In the street, following a stop and search.
2. At the police station, where they may have gone to assist with enquiries.
3. At work, home, youth club or school. However, young people under 17 should not be arrested at school unless this is unavoidable, and when this happens the head must be informed. Heads are very loath to allow this without parents being informed.

Arrest without a warrant
The police have the power to arrest anyone who is committing a breach of the peace – they do not need a warrant to do this. A breach of the peace can be any form of disturbance which harms someone or their property, or is likely to harm or cause them to be afraid.

The Public Order Act 1986 gives the police other powers of arrest without a warrant. it allows a policeman who may not be in uniform to arrest someone whom they reasonably suspect is using threatening behaviour or abusive or insulting words, or who may be violent towards another person.

Another more controversial power is that the police can arrest without warrant for what is known as offensive conduct. This relates to offences where insulting or threatening behaviour is carried out within the hearing of someone and causes them distress. This relies more on the police's interpretation of what may or may not be happening. It is supposed to cover incidents such as young people causing disturbances in blocks of flats, peering through windows, knocking over dustbins, but it can also cover annoying people at bus stops or waiting in the cinema queue.

Arrest with a warrant

The police will go to a magistrate and ask for a warrant to arrest someone if:

1. That person has failed to go to court following a summons.
2. They have not reported to the police station to answer bail.
3. A serious offence has been committed.

If the police approach you or come to your home and say that they have a warrant for your arrest, you or your parents should ask to see it and check that you are the person named or described on it. You should also note the date that it was issued, the offence, and the name of the officer that it has been issued to. You should also check on the back of the warrant to see if it has been endorsed, i.e. 'backed' for bail; this means that the person arrested will be released by the police as long as they agree to go to court when they are asked.

What should happen when you are arrested

If the police arrest you they should make very clear what
is happening. They do not have to use any particular form
of words; however, they must explain that they are
placing you under restraint and that you are being given
no choice other than to go with them. The police must also
tell you why you are being arrested, and must caution you,
saying that you do not have to say anything unless you
wish to do so, but that whatever you do say may be given
in evidence. Once you have been arrested you are no
longer free to come and go as you please, until the police
decide to release you.

If you are not already at the police station you should
be taken there as soon as possible.

Visiting or searching a place where you may be arrested

The police may search premises where they have gone to
arrest someone. They can also ask magistrates for a
warrant to enter and search the premises, although they
will not be granted a search and entry warrant without
satisfying the magistrates that their information is
accurate.

The police prefer to search with you or your parents'
consent, even if they have a warrant. If they do not have a
warrant they can search with your consent, first telling
you why they are searching, that any items seized can be
used as evidence, whether or not you are a suspect, and
that you do not have to agree to the search. If they take
anything away they will give you a receipt and they should
make a record of the search.

AT THE POLICE STATION

No one who is a juvenile, that is under 17 years old, can
be interviewed in the police station or in their home
without an appropriate adult being present. The
appropriate adult can be a parent or whoever looks after

you, or someone from social services if you are in care, or a
social worker; it can be any adult who knows you, such as
a youth leader, or anyone except a member of the police
force or a civilian employed by the police, unless they
happen to be your parents.

When a young person goes to the police station they
may not have been arrested – they may be going
voluntarily. If they are going to be interviewed by the
police, then the appropriate adult must also be present.
And if the police have to wait until that person can be
found and arrives at the police station, then they cannot
put the young person into a cell unless there is no
alternative, and then never in a cell with an adult
detainee. Wherever the young person is kept they should
be regularly inspected to see that they are all right.

The first person you should see if you are taken to the
police station is the custody officer, who is responsible for
and keeps a record of everything that happens to each
detainee held at the police station.

Everyone who is arrested will be searched at the police
station, regardless of whether they have already been
searched elsewhere. A list will be made of all your
possessions and they will be removed. Items such as keys,
money and even clothing may be taken; for example, if
the police feel that you might try to harm yourself, they
may take away clothing such as a scarf or a belt. The
custody officer will then tell you you have the right:

1. To tell someone of your arrest, by telephone or by
    writing a note.
2. To see a solicitor (see Legal Aid, page 86).
3. To a copy of the custody record.
4. To see the codes of practice covering police procedure.
5. To remind you that you do not have to say anything
    unless you wish to.

When the appropriate adult arrives the police must again,
in their presence, tell the young person detained about the
right to representation, to tell someone where they are,

about the codes of practice and the custody record, why they are being detained and read the caution.

If you need medical treatment then a police surgeon or a doctor should be called. If there is a need to search you intimately then a police officer can do this in the presence of the appropriate adult, unless the young person objects to the adult being present. It is also up to the police doctor to decide that someone is unfit to be interviewed, because of drink, drugs or injuries. Intimate searches may only be conducted if an officer of the rank of superintendent or above sanctions it, and such a search would only be conducted by a doctor or a nurse. If the police believe a drug is being concealed, then a search can only take place on medical premises.

Interviews and statements

A juvenile can be interviewed without a solicitor being present, but the appropriate adult must be there. However it is always best to have a solicitor there since they will be able to advise as to whether questions should be answered. An interview is to get the detainee's version of the facts, not to make them plead guilty. Only urgent interviews may be conducted without an adult being present; such an interview would have to be authorised by a senior officer, the rank of superintendent or above, and only if they feel that delay would result in the immediate risk of harm to people or serious loss or damage to property.

The interview room must be well lit and ventilated. If someone is deaf or has difficulty speaking English then an interpreter or signer must be found. If you have not seen a solicitor before the interview begins you can ask for the interview to stop at any time to consult one. If you did ask for a solicitor to be present then they must be allowed to stay throughout the interview.

The police are allowed to ask questions that they consider relevant, but if they reach a point where they think that they have enough information to allow them to make a charge, they have to stop. So if you admit 'Yes, I was there/did take the bag/drive the car', then the interview should stop and you should be formally charged. Once this stage has been reached the police cannot ask you any more questions.

During the interview one policeman will ask the questions and another will write them down, together with your answers. Every detail must be recorded – who was present, times, breaks taken, and whether the person detained refused to sign the record of the interview. Any refusal to answer a question would be noted. The written record of an interview must then be signed by the officer conducting it, and you must be allowed to read, alter and then sign the record. If someone cannot read or write, then it must be read to them by an adult or a solicitor and any mark witnessed. Any solicitor or appropriate adult who is present should also sign.

Tape recordings

Tape recordings are now used to record interviews. You must be told if your interview is going to be taped, and you have the right to object. The taped interview should be conducted in the same way as described above. At the conclusion the tape must be removed from the recorder, sealed in your presence and marked with an exhibit label which must be signed by you and the policeman conducting the interview. The appropriate adult will also be asked to sign. If a solicitor is present, they can also sign.

You may also offer to make a statement. This you can write yourself or have written by an officer who is not allowed to change anything. You will then sign it as correct.

Identification parades

You can ask the police to be part of an identification parade, but they cannot insist that you join one. If you do agree, your solicitor and the appropriate adult should be present. If the police wish to hold an identity parade then you should take advice from a solicitor before agreeing.

Fingerprints

Once you are over 10 years old the police can take your fingerprints, providing they have reasonable suspicion of your part in a crime. These fingerprint records will be destroyed if you are not charged.

Photographs

These cannot be taken without your consent unless there are very special circumstances – the police cannot force you to be photographed.

GOING TO COURT

After you have been interviewed and charged by the police various things may happen.

1. The police may say that the charge against you is so serious that you will be kept in custody and taken to court as soon as possible.
2. You may be charged and then released on bail and told to report to the police again, say the next day.
3. You could be charged and released to await a summons telling you when to go to court.
4. If the police want to make further enquiries, they may give you a written notice telling you to come back to the police station at a later date.
5. The police may take no further action.
6. The police may decide to caution you formally.

Cautioning

After talking with social services, your school and other welfare agencies, the police may decide not to bring you to court, even though you may have admitted committing an offence. Increasingly the police are using a formal caution for offenders between the ages of 10 and 17 years, as the rate of re-offence is lower in youngsters who do not go to court. However, the police are not allowed to administer a caution unless you admit the offence.

This caution is a formal warning given by a senior police officer and reminds the young person that they could have been prosecuted in court and that further offences will result in prosecution. In some parts of the country liaison with welfare agencies has led to young people who are cautioned becoming involved with various youth activities; if properly supervised these have become a valuable alternative to an appearance in court.

Appearing in court

If you are charged by the police and then released on bail, you will be given a charge sheet which will tell you when you should report back to the police station. If you receive a summons through the post it will tell you when you have to appear in court; as well as telling you the time to report, it will also tell you where to go.

The first time you are summonsed to court you will appear in the local juvenile court if you are under 17. If you are over 17 you will have to appear before the local adult magistrates' court. Make sure that you make a note of the day and time, as failing to turn up at either the magistrates court or the police station is a separate offence, will get you into more trouble and you will be arrested for failing to appear at court.

If you have already seen a solicitor in the police station you may have decided that you would like them to represent you when you go to court. You may need to go and see them in their office before the court case so that you can discuss the case with them. If you still need to see a solicitor you are not obliged to see the same one that you saw at the police station. If you get to the court and still want to speak to a solicitor, try and speak to the duty solicitor. (For more information about using solicitors see Legal aid later in this chapter.)

You should try to get to the court early. Look for an enquiry window or desk, where there will be a court usher. Court ushers normally wear black gowns. They will check your name on the court list, tell you where to wait and which court you will go to when it is your turn to appear.

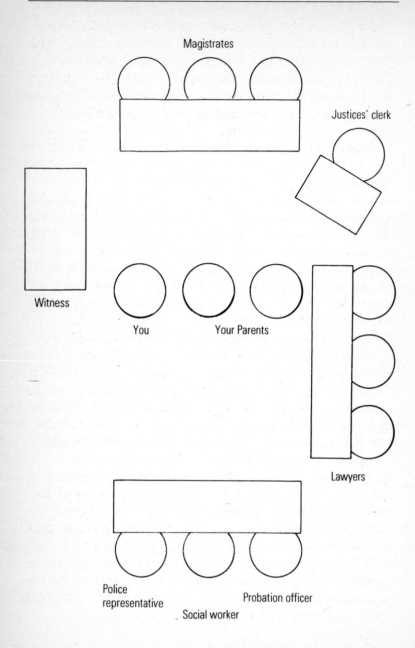

Magistrates

Justices' clerk

Witness

You

Your Parents

Lawyers

Police representative

Social worker

Probation officer

A plan of a typical juvenile court

Your parents should try and go with you. If you are in
care then someone from the social services should go with
you. If they cannot go, try and get an adult friend to wait
with you and get permission to go into the court with you.
Be prepared to wait some time before you are called; some
magistrates courts have a place where you can buy a
drink while you are waiting.

When you are finally called into the court the usher will
show you and your parents where to stand. In front of you
will be a long table or desk on a raised platform; this is
where the magistrates will be sitting. Magistrates are
members of the local community appointed by the Lord
Chancellor to hear cases in local magistrates courts. In the
juvenile court there will be three magistrates sitting, and
there must always be one man and one woman. These
magistrates are not paid, although in some of the very
busy inner city courts the magistrates will be legally
trained and paid – these are called stipendiary
magistrates and they can hear cases on their own.

After a while the magistrates will ask you to sit.
However, if you are not sure what to do, remain standing
or watch what your solicitor does. As well as places for you
and the magistrates to sit, there will be a desk or table for
solicitors and the Crown Prosecutor, and somewhere for
the police, social workers and probation officers to sit.
Members of the public are not allowed to sit in the
juvenile court, which is why your friends may not be
allowed to go in with you. Local newspaper reporters are
allowed to sit in the juvenile court, but they are not
allowed to print your name or anything about you so that
you could be recognised in a newspaper report.

There will also be the court clerk. He or she is legally
qualified and is there to advise the magistrates on the law.
The clerk will sit either to one side of the magistrates table
or immediately in front of them.

Pleading guilty or not guilty

The court clerk will read out the charge against you. They
must do this in simple terms, and you should always say if

you do not understand. You will be asked whether you plead guilty or not guilty, that is that you did or did not do it. At this stage you can do one of three things:

1. You can ask for an adjournment, that is a delay while you discuss with your solicitor what you are going to say.
2. You can plead not guilty. This means that the hearing of the case will be put off for a time while both you and the prosecutor arrange for witnesses to be present.
3. You can plead guilty, that is admit you did it. The magistrates will not accept your plea unless they are sure that you understand what you are saying. If they do accept your plea they may decide what to do with you there and then, or they may ask you to come back in a few weeks time when they have found out more about you. (See Sentencing, below.)

Hearing the evidence

If you decide to plead not guilty and have to come back to court another day, you will again have to come early and wait about. When the case is heard, first the Crown Prosecutor will set out all the evidence and call witnesses to try and convince the magistrates that you are guilty. The witnesses will tell the court what they saw or what they heard you say. If you disagree with what they say do not call out, but make sure that your solicitor knows that you don't agree. Your solicitor will have a chance to ask any questions of any of the witnesses on your behalf; this is called cross examining.

When the Crown Prosecutor has finished it will be your solicitor's turn to put your side of the story. He may do this by asking you questions, as well as calling other witnesses. Like all the other witnesses, you will be asked to take an oath of your own faith that you will tell the truth. If you have no faith then you will be asked to affirm, that is promise to tell the truth. When you are answering any questions, either from your solicitor or the Crown Prosecutor, look at the magistrates. Speak clearly and don't try to hurry. If the magistrates ask you a question, stand up straight and answer clearly. Always address the magistrates as 'Sir' or 'Madam'.

If there is someone who is prepared to come to court to speak on your behalf because they know you, let your solicitor know in advance that they would like to speak. They are called character witnesses.

After you and any witnesses called on your behalf have given evidence, then you or your solicitor can make a closing statement to the court, summarising your case.

The magistrates' decision

When the magistrates have heard all the evidence, they will probably retire – leave the court – while they make their decision. Everyone in the court will be told to stand when they leave and when they return. You will also have to stand while they give the decision.

They may decide that you are not guilty or that the case is not proved. This means that you are free to leave the court.

If they find you guilty, or you have pleaded guilty, at this point the Crown Prosecutor will tell the court if you have any previous convictions or formal cautions. Again, if you disagree with what he is saying you should let your solicitor know straight away.

Even though you have been found guilty you may not be told what is to happen to you. This is because the magistrates will ask for reports on you, your family and your school life before sentencing you. The social worker or the probation officer will be asked to prepare the reports, and you will all have to come back again after one or two weeks. This will involve you visiting the social worker or probation officer, and possibly their coming to your home. When this happens don't forget to say all the positive things about yourself, and again mention all those people who are prepared to speak on your behalf.

In most cases, though, the report will have been prepared before you appear in court, which means that the magistrates will be able to sentence you there and then.

SENTENCING IN A MAGISTRATES COURT

Your solicitor should try to see copies of any reports, so that you can challenge anything that may be inaccurate. The magistrates will read the reports, and may ask you some questions. They will also ask your parents if they want to say anything. Your solicitor will use these reports, as well as the statements of any character witnesses, to ask for a lighter sentence. This is called a plea in mitigation.

When the magistrates have read all the reports and listened to your solicitor they will finally make a decision. In sentencing you, they will take into account any previous sentences that you may have served. This generally means that the more times you appear in court the stiffer your sentence will be each time.

Absolute or conditional discharge

If the magistrates decide that, in spite of your being found guilty, what you have done is a very minor matter then they can give you an absolute discharge. This means that although you have a conviction against you there will be no punishment.

A conditional discharge means that you will not receive any punishment now but if you are convicted again within a certain period – say three years – any punishment for this offence will be added on. It is a way of putting you on trust as to your future behaviour.

Bindover

If you are bound over to keep the peace you will have to sign an undertaking that you will behave for up to one year. If you break the agreement you will have to pay the sum of money shown in the agreement. Similarly your parents can be asked to take proper care of you and to exercise control, and they will have to pay a sum of money if you get into further trouble.

Fines, costs and compensation

In the cases of a fine, costs or compensation, either you or your parents can be ordered to pay money to the court or to another person.

1. Fines are a direct punishment, up to a maximum of £100 for a 10–13 year old and £400 for a 14–16 year old.
2. Costs will be a sum of money to pay to the court for the court's costs.
3. Compensation may be awarded by the court to be paid by you to the victim of your crime; for example, for any damage that may be caused.

If you are under 17 and are fined or ordered to pay compensation, then your parents will be ordered to pay the money required, unless they cannot be found or the magistrates feel that it would be unreasonable to make your parents pay because of the circumstances of the case.

Endorsement and disqualification

If you have been convicted of a road traffic offence your driving licence may be endorsed with a number of penalty points. If you do not have a licence and get one later, then the licence you get will have the endorsements and penalty points recorded on it. You may also be disqualified from driving over a period of time, and this may happen even if, at the time you appear in court, you are too young to drive.

Supervision order

The court may decide that you are in need of a supervision order. This means that you will be 'assisted, advised and befriended' by a social worker or, sometimes, a probation officer for up to three years. Whoever supervises you will organise some of your activities and keep an eye on your behaviour. You must tell this supervisor if you change your address.

Intermediate treatment (IT) or supervised activity

This is a form of supervision order, with special conditions. The IT scheme is organised by local authorities and provides activities for you for up to a total of 90 days. You may have to take part in community activities, go to sports activities or join a youth club. There may be restrictions placed on you, as to when you can go out at night or at weekends. What you do depends on your supervisor, again a social worker or probation officer.

Attendance centre orders

You may be ordered to go to an attendance centre for up to 24 hours in all. Most attendance centres are run by the police with the social services department. They operate on a Saturday morning or afternoon. Again there will be organised activities such as sports or crafts.

Community service

These orders are made for 16 year olds who have committed serious crimes. You will be asked to do unpaid community work for between 40 and 120 hours. This work must not interfere with school or work, nor conflict with your religious beliefs. The work should be undertaken within a year, but if it isn't the order will stay in force until the hours are completed. If an order is breached then you can be fined up to £200 or given another sentence.

Care orders

If a young person between the ages of 10–16 years commits a serious crime they can be made the subject of a care order. This means that the local social services department becomes responsible for your welfare. Although you may live in a children's home or be fostered with another family, you may still be allowed to visit your parents, unless the court forbids it or advises otherwise or you commit another offence.

Detention in a young offender's institution

If you have committed a serious offence, and have been in trouble before, you may be given a custodial sentence. However, it is generally accepted by government that custody should be seen as a last resort, and used only when the young person is unwilling or unable to respond to non-custodial penalties, that custody is necessary for the protection of the public, or the offence is so serious that there is no alternative to a custodial sentence.

You cannot be given a custodial sentence if you are under 14. The minimum sentence is normally 21 days, and you cannot be sent away for longer than 12 months. You will be entitled to remission of one half of the sentence, which means that you will only serve half the time imposed unless you abscond or break the rules.

Committal for sentence in a Crown Court

If a young person over 15 is found guilty of a serious offence by the magistrates, they may send him or her to the Crown Court for sentencing if the magistrates feel that he or she should be sentenced to a period of longer than 12 months.

Deferred sentences

The court may decide that they will not sentence you for up to six months but will watch your behaviour during this time before deciding what action to take. At the end of that time you will go back to court and they will decide how to deal with you on the basis of how you have behaved during the six months.

SERIOUS CRIMES

For very serious crimes like arson, rape or robbery, where the magistrates consider that you should be sent away for more than two years, you may be sent to the Crown Court for trial, and be given a longer sentence than could be ordered by the magistrates.

If you are charged with murder, you must be sent to the

Crown Court for trial. If convicted you will be detained for an unlimited period and you would only be released when the Home Secretary decides it is appropriate.

APPEALING AGAINST A SENTENCE

If you are unhappy about the sentence imposed upon you by the magistrates, you can appeal to the Crown Court. However, if you decide to do this you must send a notice to the magistrates clerk within 21 days of the decision being made.

If your case was heard in the Crown Court, then you can appeal to the Court of Appeal in London, although the Court of Appeal will only change a sentence if it feels that it was unduly harsh or wrongly imposed.

LEGAL AID

If your case was heard in the Crown Court, then you can appeal to the Court of Appeal in London, although the trouble with the police; you may also need legal advice if you are going into care, or you have a problem with a landlord. Ask your local Citizen's Advice Bureau which solicitors can offer you specialist advice, to check whether you would be eligible for legal aid and if local solicitors can offer any free or inexpensive advice.

There are several different ways of getting legal advice.

Free legal advice

If you live near a law centre or Citizen's Advice Bureau you may have access to a solicitor without any charge. Local law centres are staffed by lawyers, and Citizen's Advice Bureaux often have free sessions one day a week, although this would only be for general advice.

Fixed fee interview

A fixed fee interview will give you half an hour's advice for £5 including VAT. It is not means tested, so everyone pays £5. However, it is only an interview. A solicitor will not be able to do anything more than advise you, but fixed fee interviews are a good way of finding out if you need to have a solicitor to act for you.

Not all solicitors will give fixed fee interviews. Your local Citizen's Advice Bureau will know which solicitors do.

Duty solicitor scheme

Duty solicitors are available to advise anyone in police custody. There is no charge for this service. The police are obliged to tell you that you are entitled to have legal advice and that, if you do not know the name of a solicitor, they will arrange for you to see one. They do not choose the solicitor for you; the solicitors are organised by local duty solicitor committees.

As well as providing solicitors to go to the police stations, they also arrange for solicitors to be available at magistrates court, so that anyone can get advice before their case is heard. They can also represent you briefly in court.

The Green Form Scheme

The Green Form Scheme allows people to get a variety of services from a solicitor. The solicitor will be able to write letters, negotiate on their client's behalf, etc. If more work needs to be done the solicitor will need to get permission from the Law Society. Furthermore the solicitor cannot represent a client in court under the Green Form Scheme.

Qualifying for free advice and help on the Green Form Scheme depends on whether you have any income or savings. Your solicitor works this out for you using a scale of allowances and then fills in a green form, hence the name of the scheme. Once you are 16 years old you can apply for aid under this scheme for yourself and it is your earnings and savings that will be assessed. If you are under 16 an adult can apply on your behalf, the solicitor will assess the income and savings of whichever adult is responsible for you. It can be your parents, but if they refuse to be assessed then the solicitor can assess your income and savings instead.

Criminal legal aid

Criminal legal aid is available to a young person who is being charged with a criminal offence, and is also available for a young person who is subject to care proceedings as a result of a criminal offence. A young person is able to ask for a solicitor without the help of an adult. Criminal legal aid will cover the cost of preparing a case and representation in court. In serious cases legal aid can also cover the appointment of a barrister, as well as any necessary appeal after sentencing.

You can apply for legal aid yourself or, if you are under 17, your parents can apply on your behalf. The final decision to award criminal legal aid lies with the court, who have to decide whether or not the case merits its award.

Civil legal aid

You will need to use civil legal aid if you are involved in care proceedings. Young people under the age of 16 years cannot apply for legal aid – an adult has to do it for them. If the young person is bringing the case then the adult will be called a 'next friend' or a guardian *ad litem* (see Care proceedings, page 42). As with Green Form advice, there will be an assessment of any income or savings that you might have.

Where you might gain financially from winning a case helped by civil legal aid then the Law Society, who administer the Legal Aid Fund, will ask for some of its money back. This is called a statutory charge and will be deducted from any money or settlement that you win.

7.
WHEN YOU DECIDE TO LEAVE HOME

My mum wants to throw me out, there's not enough room at home and everybody fights. She says that as I've got a job I can go and rent a room somewhere. I'm 17 and have a job, but I don't earn much money. Would the council let me rent or do I have to try one of the local landlords?

You may need to leave home for a variety of reasons. You may be going because of a job, college placement or training course; it may be that things are difficult at home and you want to leave; or your parents may want you to leave or may even throw you out.

There are several things you need to be sure about if you have to leave home:

1. Can your parents or guardians do anything to prevent you going?
2. Where are you going to live and will you be safe?
3. What money are you going to live on?

CAN YOU LEAVE HOME?

Young people under the age of 18 need their parents' consent to leave home unless they are married. If a young person between 16 and 18 leaves home without their parents' consent the police or social services are unlikely to step in, but there are legal remedies that the parents can use to make a young person return.

For example, they can ask that you be made a ward of

court, which means that the High Court will take over all parental responsibilities for you. But the court will not just do what your parents want; the Court is bound to take into account your wishes and feelings, particularly if you are over 16.

Alternatively your parents may ask the social services to intervene. They have a number of powers they can exercise, as well as offering advice and support to both you and your parents. If they feel that you are at risk in any way they may make use of a care or supervision order. Again they are bound to take your needs and wishes into consideration. (See Chapter 3, When things go wrong in the family.)

YOUNG PEOPLE UNDER 18

If you are under 18 your parents have a responsibility to care and provide a home for you. If you decide to leave or they throw you out either you or they can approach the social services and ask for suitable arrangements to be sorted out. If you are the one who makes the decision but you don't want to go to the social services, try making an approach through your school or a trusted friend. Schools have a responsibility to assist you, particularly if you are at risk.

Social services will take your wishes into consideration and there are a number of options open to both you and your parents if there is a chance of negotiation or reconciliation. They may suggest some sort of temporary arrangement such as staying with relatives or friends to provide a breathing space, or reorganising the living space at home so that individual members of the family have more privacy. If none of these solutions are appropriate, or have previously failed, they can, if you are under 16, take you into care.

Can your parents tell you to leave?
Remember that, although your parents have a responsibility to care and provide a home for you if you

are under 16, you have no right in law to live in your
parents' home. Your parents can ask you to leave, but if
they do so they must give you notice. As we have already
seen there are various options open to you through the
social services, which may range from fostering and care
orders to sponsoring of accommodation in rented property
or a hostel.

If your parents are married then either one can tell you
to leave. If the adults you live with are not married but
cohabiting, i.e. seen to be living together as man and wife,
then only the one who owns the house or, in the case of
rented property, whose name is on the rent book can ask
you to leave. In such circumstances a cohabiting parent
may find themselves torn between protecting their son or
daughter or having to side with their cohabitee and ask
their child to leave; this can occur where a woman with
children lives with a man, in his house, and he wants one
of the children to leave – it is his house, so he can. If it
were her house it would be up to her to make the decision,
but she may find it difficult to resist her partner's wishes,
particularly if he has a forceful personality or is the main
wage earner.

Other reasons for needing housing

If you are staying in someone else's house, say with
friends or relatives, you are unlikely to be able to stay if
they ask you to leave unless you have a formal agreement
with them or a tenancy with your name on the rent book.

If, for example, you are pregnant and are under 18,
while you may not take up much room during your
pregnancy, once the baby arrives there may be
considerable strain on the space available in the house. If
you are asked to leave in these circumstances you will
have to check to see if the local council are able to re-
house you under the Housing (Homeless Persons) Act.
The council may insist that you be allowed to stay at
home for the moment to give them more time to sort
things out, and they may also insist that you are given
notice in writing.

And do not assume that being accepted for re-housing by a council is the end of all your problems. Different local councils interpret the law on housing homeless people in many ways and often the accommodation they provide is not suitable.

If you don't fit into any of these situations – maybe you just want or need to leave home – where do you start looking for somewhere to live?

HOUSING

Finding somewhere to live is probably one of the most difficult tasks that anyone, not just people under 18, face. Whether you are buying a home, renting a flat or bedsit or just trying to get into a hostel or bed and breakfast accommodation, there are difficulties. This is simply because there is a shortage of decent accommodation; what there is is expensive, and those looking often don't have enough, or indeed any, money. The reason that tens of thousands of people in this country won't have a place to sleep tonight, or any night, is that they can't find the housing and they don't have the money.

So, if you have left home what choices are open to you?

Buying a home
Under the age of 18 you cannot own property, although it can be held in trust for you.

While you are under 18 you are not going to get a mortgage – borrow money for a house. Once you are 18 you can apply for a mortgage, but banks and building societies are looking for reliability, which in their terms means someone with a steady income who can make the repayments. Not many of these institutions will lend you the full value of a house – a 100 per cent mortgage – so you will also need considerable savings. Buying a house is thus a long term proposition.

Renting from your local authority

Local authorities – 'the council' – have a responsibility to house certain groups of people, or anyone who has been on their housing list for a certain length of time. To climb a council's waiting list you gain points, which are allocated to you depending on your particular situation.

As a rule young people are given very few points and are not quickly housed, unless they live in an area where the council has decided that young people are vulnerable under the Housing (Homeless Persons) Act. This Act obliges councils to find accommodation, not necessarily houses or flats, for people who are in priority need, perhaps because they are:

1. Pregnant.
2. Homeless after an emergency such as a fire.
3. Vulnerable because of mental illness, physical handicap or disability, or for any special reason such as alcoholism or drug addiction.

So, despite the law saying that every application for housing should be looked at separately, just being young, single and homeless is not enough.

Councils do not normally accept people under the age of 18 as tenants unless they have a guarantor for the rent, in the event of rent arrears. People who are sponsored in this way tend to be placed by either social services or the probation service. You will even find it difficult to put your name on the council list while you are under 18.

Councils should offer you advice about housing, but you may find that this will only be a list of bed and breakfast hotels and housing associations. Even if you are accepted as needing housing, you will probably be put into either accommodation that no one else wants or into a bed and breakfast hotel.

Renting from housing associations

Housing associations also have properties for rent. They are privately run, although often financially supported by

government together with a local or national charity. They
also have their list of priorities and may restrict
themselves to letting to older people, families with
children or young people. They have waiting lists and also
want guarantees for the rent before renting to young
people.

Renting from private landlords

By looking in your local paper or using an accommodation
agency you will see what property is available for rent in
your area. The problem will be that rents in the private
sector will be higher than those charged by a local council
or housing association. Landlords may also be reluctant to
let to under 18s because of the difficulties in enforcing
rent arrears and other conditions of the tenancy, and you
nay have difficulty in finding the rent in advance that
landlords want. If you are using an accommodation
agency they ask you for a fee just to be on their books.
Requesting these sums of money is illegal, but in a
situation where suitable housing is scarce you may be
tempted to do anything that gives you some advantage
over other people in the queue.

Local housing advice centres and Citizen's Advice
Bureaux can advise you about local landlords, particularly
if they are 'difficult'. They may also have lists on notice
boards of rooms or flats to let or share. Otherwise you can
try all the local newsagents and community centres in the
area where you want to live to see whether they have
cards detailing people offering rooms.

If you do find somewhere to rent or to share, make sure
before you hand over any money or sign anything that you
have the agreement checked by your local housing advice
centre, law centre or Citizen's Advice Bureau. The copy of
your agreement or lease should tell you:

1. What your rent is and how it should be paid, i.e.
    weekly, monthly, personally to the landlord or through
    the bank.
2. What the rent covers. Are charges for water, gas,

electricity, rates and telephone paid separately or
included, for example?

3. When the landlord wants to visit.
4. What repairs and decorations are your responsibility
and what the landlord will undertake to do.
5. An inventory of all the furniture, crockery, bedding,
etc., in the house.
6. Any restrictions placed on you, such as no pets,
sticking pictures on the wall, etc.

Changes in the housing law in January 1989 have created
new tenancies. If you are a new or an existing tenant and
you are offered a new agreement, do check with your local
Citizen's Advice Bureau or housing advice centre to see
how these changes affect you. Usually tenants pay the
costs of drawing up such agreements.

Hostels

Like housing associations, these may be run by charities
or management committees who decide who the hostel
should be for, e.g. unmarried mothers, homeless men,
former offenders, rehabilitating alcoholics or drug users.
The good ones are always full, but if you are leaving home
for the first time they can be a bridge between being at
home and being completely independent. There will be
rules about the hours for being in, when you are allowed to
have visitors, when you can play radios, etc., in your
rooms. Charges will differ, depending on the facilities
available.

Bed and breakfast hotels

The traditional lodgings where you were looked after by a
landlady have almost disappeared. Present-day bed and
breakfast hotels are just that – you have a bed in a single
or shared room and after breakfast you leave and you may
not be allowed to go back again until the evening. This
may be fine when you are on holiday, but if you are
unemployed and it's raining it's not much fun. Again

housing advice centres and Citizen's Advice Bureaux will have local lists.

Squatting

If you can make your way in to a property without doing any damage, and providing no one else has the use of it as a home, then you are not committing a crime. But if you are under 18 your parents may use the fact that you are squatting to say that you are in danger, and ask the social services to take responsibility for you. If you have no alternative but to squat take advice from either your local housing advice centre or Citizen's Advice Bureau or, if you live in London, from the Advisory Centre for Squatters (see Useful addresses) and try to get hold of a copy of the *Squatters Handbook* from them.

Staying with friends or relatives

Often this is a temporary solution that you can use when you first leave home. You parents will know where you are, it's not unlike being at home, your meals are cooked, your washing is done for you. But it is rarely a permanent arrangement. Other members of the family may need your room, you may find it too restrictive – too much like home!

If the family concerned are on benefit or on low earnings it may be that whatever money you give them does not make up for the adjustments to the losses in their income support or housing benefit.

HOUSING BENEFIT

So the housing maze is difficult to negotiate, and your problems will be compounded if you haven't much money, even if you are earning or on YTS. So are there any benefits that you can claim?

Housing benefit is to help you pay your rent and rates if your earnings are low. You can also get housing benefit if you are on income support, but the rules for under 18s claiming income support are now very restricted (see below). If you are working but earning very little, or on

YTS, you should be able to claim some housing benefit.

Housing benefit is available to anyone over the age of 16 who is responsible for their own housing costs. It covers rent and rates, but only that part of the rent that is to pay for being in the house or flat and not for any other charges that may be included. You cannot claim housing benefit for mortgage payments; these are dealt with by the DSS under income support.

Housing benefit is administered by the local authority – 'the council'. To claim you go to the council offices and ask for a claim form. If you are a student the rules for claiming are slightly different, so read the section on students if this applies to you.

If you are not sure about whether you should claim housing benefit or whether it has been worked out correctly, then check with your local housing advice centre, Citizen's Advice Centre or Young People's Advisory Service. They can work out if it is worth your claiming if you tell them your circumstances.

What the council need to know
In deciding whether or not to pay you housing benefit the council will need to know:

1. How much rent and rates you pay.
2. How much you earn or receive in training allowances.
3. Whether someone else shares the accommodation with you. If you are living in a flat or house and share with other people you will only be allowed to claim for a proportion of the rent and rates. But if you live in a house that is divided into a number of separate flats or bedsits and you do not share your particular room or flat with anyone, then you will have all your rent and rates included in the assessment.
4. Who is your landlord? They will not be willing to let you have housing benefit if they feel that the tenancy has been contrived just to get housing benefit; an example of this would be if you rented from a close relative.

If you are in doubt always check with your local housing advice centre or Citizen's Advice Bureau.

Housing benefit calculation

Once the council know your rent and your earnings they will first work out what is known as your applicable amount. This is done by using a series of premiums and allowances determined annually by Parliament, based on your age, your marital status, whether you have any children, or have any serious disability. They will then compare your applicable amount with your weekly income. If your income is less than your applicable amount, then you will get the maximum entitlement to housing benefit, which is all of your rent and 80 per cent of your rates.

If your income is more than your applicable amount, then for every £1 that your income is over they will reduce your housing benefit by 65p for rent and 20p for rates. Here is an example:

John is 17 and earns £47.40 a week after deductions. Every week he pays £20 rent and £5 rates. His personal allowance for someone under the age of 18 is £27.40 (April 1989). He is not eligible for any premiums as he is fit, and has no wife or child. So his applicable amount is £27.40.

His earnings	£47.40
are more than his applicable amount	27.40
	£20.00

His maximum theoretical housing benefit would be:

Rent	£20.00
80 per cent of rates (80% × £5)	4.00
	£24.00

But this will be reduced by 65p for every £1 (i.e. 65 per cent) of earnings for rent and 20p for every £1 (i.e. 20

per cent) of earnings for rates. So John's housing
benefit calculation looks like this:

Excess income £20.00
Maximum rent   £20.00
   less 65% × £20   13.00

Housing benefit for rent   £7.00
Maximum allowed rates   £4.00
   less 20% × £20   4.00

Housing benefit for rates   nil

Total housing benefit   £7.00

So John will only pay £13 (£20—£7) of his original rent
and because his excess income is too large, he will get no
help with his rates.

Indeed if housing benefit for either rent or rates works out
at less than 50p in either case, then no benefit will be paid.

Savings
If you have savings of between £3,000 and £8,000 there
will be assumed income from these savings which will be
added to your weekly income. If you have more than
£8,000 in savings, regardless of how little you earn you
will not be able to claim housing benefit.

How you will be paid
If you qualify for housing benefit, then the council will
send you a cheque so that you continue to pay your
landlord the full rent. If you are one of the exceptional
group of under 18s housed by the council, then they will
adjust your rent book.

Unreasonable rents
If the council think that your rent is too high then they
will only allow a reasonable amount to be assessed for
housing benefit. They may also refuse you if they think
that the accommodation is unsuitable.

INCOME SUPPORT

Since September 1988 most 16 and 17 year olds leaving
school will not be able to claim income support. This is
because government has said that for every young person
unemployed and available for work there will be a place
on a Youth Training Scheme and so there will be no
reason for any young person to be unemployed. However,
even though you have left school, your parents may still
be able to continue to get child benefit for you for a short
time. This depends upon when you leave school, so check
with your local Young People's Advisory Service or
Citizen's Advice bureau.

Some 16 and 17 year olds will still be able to claim
income support. This is because they would not normally
have to be available for work and therefore they would not
be obliged to take up a YTS place. They are:

1. Single parents.
2. Some couples married or living together with a child.
3. Pregnant women – exemption begins 11 weeks before
   the baby is due and continues for 7 weeks after the
   baby is born.
4. Registered blind people.
5. People whose mental and physical disability means
   that they are unlikely to find work within 12 months.
6. Carers for people receiving attendance allowance.
7. People temporarily laid off.
8. Some refugees and those seeking asylum.

If you are on YTS you will receive a training allowance
(see page 61); if you have other expenses not covered by
your training allowance or any accommodation given to
you, you may be able to get help from the DSS.

If for any other reason you are living away from home
and waiting to be placed on YTS, you may get income
support for a short while. For example:

1. You have no living parent or guardian.

2. You have been in the care of the local authority for the last two years.
3. You are under the supervision of a social worker or a probation officer or you are on bail.
4. You cannot live at home because of the threat of physical or sexual abuse.
5. Your parents are in prison, in a home or hospital or abroad and cannot return (but not serving in the forces).
6. You are estranged from your parents; this means that you are unable to go back home.

And if you fit into one of the following groups you will get income support for a limited period.

1. For summer school leavers until 31 December.
2. For Christmas school leavers until 12 weeks from the first Monday in January.
3. For Easter school leavers for 12 weeks after the first Monday after Easter Sunday.

If at the end of this time you are ill and cannot take up your YTS placement then benefit may continue until you are fit.

Unavoidable severe hardship

If you don't fit into any of the groups already mentioned, you will have to show that you would suffer unavoidable severe hardship in order to claim income support. A decision about this would not be taken by a local DSS but by the Secretary of State for Social Security (although in practice this merely means that another DSS civil servant makes the decision). Because this decision is at the discretion of a civil servant then you cannot appeal against it, only challenge the decision at a review if you can show that the DSS did not take all the relevant facts into account.

Here is an example of the benefit knot that one 16 year old found herself in:

Mary has just been thrown out by her stepfather because he has found out that she is pregnant. He refuses to have her back but there is no risk of violence or abuse within the home. Mary tried to register for YTS at the careers office. They sent her to the local course manager who said 'But you're pregnant, no one will want to employ you. Go away!' The DSS refused to accept Mary as a claimant because she is not on YTS and does not fit into any of their exceptional categories. She is under no threat of violence or abuse and, although she is pregnant, they can only consider her when it is 11 weeks prior to the birth. So she has no money.

Mary consulted her local Citizen's Advice Bureau who, like Mary, spent a long time to-ing and fro-ing between the careers office, the DSS and the local course manager. Eventually, someone in the local careers office said 'Everyone under the age of 18 is guaranteed a place on YTS' and agreed that Mary should return to the careers office and ask to be put on the Initial Training course. Therefore Mary would get YTS allowances and assistance from housing benefit until she was 29 weeks pregnant, when she could claim income support on the grounds of pregnancy. After the baby was born she could continue to claim income support for herself and the child as a single parent.

Income support and housing benefit

If you get income support and are responsible for your housing costs then you will get 100 per cent of your rent and 80 per cent of your rates paid. You will be given a form by the DSS to complete for housing benefit when you claim income support; complete the forms and return them to the DSS. If you are not sure about anything ask your local young people's advisory service or Citizen's Advice Bureau.

Board and lodging payment

From April 1989 if you are under 18 and providing you are

eligible, you will claim income support and housing benefit. So you will be assessed by the DSS for your personal needs and be given an allowance based on your personal allowance and any premiums that you qualify for. This will give you your applicable amount. For some people under 25 this will be £27.40 (in 1989). You will apply for housing benefit from the local authority and you will receive your board and lodging costs, less any amount that has been included for meals or fuel. Any income that you have will be taken into account. If you are already getting board and lodging payments you should get some protection so that you are no worse off. Check with your local Citizen's Advice Bureau or DSS to see if you have been correctly assessed.

Under 16

If you are under 16 you cannot get any benefit in your own right – your parents will get child benefit for you. This benefit does not have to cease when you are 16, but if you leave school and get a job or join YTS it stops. If you remain at school or in full-time education it can continue until you are 19.

STUDENTS AND BENEFIT

If you leave school at 16 but decide to continue studying you will find that the rules for students are just as complicated as they are for the unemployed. You will need to know:

1. How many hours you will be studying.
2. Whether your course is considered advanced or non-advanced, part time or full time. (See Chapter 2 for a definition of non-advanced education.)

To check whether you can get income support ask either your Citizen's Advice Bureau or student welfare officer who are aware of the DSS rules about different types of courses.

Grants

There are two types of grant paid by the local authority, mandatory and discretionary.

A mandatory grant is one that must be paid if you are following a certain course. You cannot get a mandatory grant if you are studying:

1. GCSEs and A levels.
2. BTEC awards, as distinct from HNC and HND courses.
3. City and Guilds courses.

However your local authority may be prepared to give you a discretionary grant. You will have to explain all your circumstances to them, and how much they will award is up to them but any award will be based on the guidelines used for the mandatory grants.

If you don't think that you will get either you can apply to the student welfare fund or ask your local reference library or Citizen's Advice Bureau whether there are any local educational charities you can ask for money. Otherwise your parents will have to continue to support you as they would have done if you had stayed at school.

Students and housing benefit

Students are able to claim housing benefit if they are responsible for their housing costs, and rent from:

1. The local authority – the council.
2. A private landlord.
3. A housing association.

A student will not get housing benefit if they live in college accommodation such as a hall of residence, although there are exceptions to this:

1. If a student is directly responsible for the rates.
2. If the hall of residence is rented from someone else.
3. If you live in a hall of residence all the year round but

any grant you receive only covers term time. Housing benefit would then be available for the summer vacation.

These circumstances would be unusual for someone under the age of 18, but if you think you may be eligible for housing benefit check with your local Citizen's Advice Bureau or housing advice centre.

This must all seem very disheartening – the reality is that there is very little support for people between 16 and 18 who want to study unless their parents can help them. But for some people it can work:

Caroline is 17 and in the sixth form at school, studying for four A levels. She lives with her mother and stepfather. Her natural father has moved to another part of the country and she doesn't see him very often.

Her mother is very aggressive towards her; Caroline can show you burn marks on her arms and scratches around her neck. Her school work is beginning to suffer, but no one at school has said anything – yet.

Can she leave home and get income support, or will she have to leave school before the DSS give her any money? Fortunately because the DSS were convinced that Caroline was suffering physical abuse from her mother they were prepared to give her income support. She also found a place in a local hostel and, with the support of her school finished her A levels.

SENDING MESSAGES HOME

If, for some reason, you have left home and don't want your parents to know where you are, but you want them to know that you are all right, then you record a message to send to your parents by ringing Message Home. This service is run by the Mother's Union, it is confidential and will not be used to trace you. Any message you leave will be passed on to your parents.

The telephone lines are available 24 hours a day, and the numbers are as follows:

Birmingham	021-426 3396
Bristol	0272 504717
Leeds	0532 454544
London	071-799 7662
Liverpool	051-709 7598
Portsmouth	0705 733899
Scotland	0968 76161

8.
WHEN YOU CAN DECIDE FOR YOURSELF

My brother and I live with my mum. She is separated from my dad, who is living abroad. She has always made a fuss if he writes to us or sends us presents, and complains that he doesn't give her enough money to keep us. In his last letter to us he said that he had enclosed a £20 note for each of us for Christmas. My mum just took the money and said that it would help to pay the bills. Can she do this or should she have given the money to us?

BUSINESS

Your parents have a general responsibility to look after your money and your property, but they have no legal right to any money or property that belongs or is given to you.

Bank accounts

A bank will let you open an account at any age. Banks have all types of current, savings and deposit accounts for young people, all promoted with a great deal of expensive publicity material and special offers such as pens, kit bags, tee shirts, etc.

Banks will also offer you a cash card for getting money from a bank's cash machine, but will probably not give you a cheque book and a cheque guarantee card if you have not left school. And they will not grant you an overdraft until you are 18, because they want to be sure of getting their money back (see Contracts and guarantees, below).

You can open an account with the Post Office Girobank once you are 15. Anyone can open a National Savings account at the post office for you, but you won't be able to take money out of it until you are 7. And when you are 7 you can open an account with the Trustee Savings Bank.

Contracts and guarantees

People under the age of 18 will find it difficult to borrow money on hire purchase or credit. This is because finance companies will want to be sure of getting their money back, and someone under 18 cannot be sued. They will therefore ask for a guarantor for someone who is under 18 before they will grant a loan. If you are going to ask your parents to act as your guarantor it means that they will be responsible for paying back the money you have borrowed if you don't or are unable to, for example if you lose your job.

A contract signed by someone under 18 can be enforced if it is agreed that it is for necessities. It is not entirely clear what necessities are, but some examples are clothes and food; expensive electrical goods are not necessities.

A piece of legislation called the Minors' Contracts Act says that where anyone makes a contract with someone under 18, and that contract is unenforceable because of the young person's age, then a court has the discretion to order the young person to return the goods.

Data on computer files

You can apply to see information about you held on computer files at any age. The only restrictions are files which are exempted by the Data Protection Act; for example, you may be refused access to police, medical, dental or social work computer records. If you think that there is information about you on a computer file, check with your local Citizen's Advice Bureau to see if you can be allowed to see what is written.

Premium Bonds

You can buy Premium Bonds yourself when you are 16.
Before that they can be bought on your behalf.

Wills and inheritance

You cannot make a will or inherit property or money until
you are 18. Anything left to you before this must be held
in trust. The exception to this is if you are a seaman or in
the armed forces you may make a will once you have
joined.

Legitimacy and illegitimacy

A child is legitimate if its father and mother were married
when it was born or conceived. Merely putting the father's
name on a birth certificate if the parents are unmarried
will not make the birth legitimate.

If your parents marry after your birth then you become
legitimate. The same applies if you are adopted
at some time before you are 18.

HEALTH

Confidential advice from a doctor

Whatever your age, you have the right to a confidential
appointment and talk with your doctor. But if you are
under 16 your doctor will always try and encourage you to
tell your parents that you have been to the doctor.

If a doctor is unwilling to give you confidential advice,
then you should consider talking to one of the counselling
agencies or to an organisation such as the Brook Advisory
Service (see Useful addresses).

Medical, dental and optical treatment.

Once you are over 16 you can give consent to your own
examination or treatment; under the age of 16 the law is
not entirely clear. Legislation assumes that consent by
someone under 16 to a medical examination would be
valid, providing they can fully understand what the

proposed treatment involves. This consent covers everything, including abortion, except experimental operations and the donation of blood or organs. To do this you must be 18.

In practice doctors will seek the consent of the parents or carer of young people under the age of 18, for treatment and operations.

Benefits

If you are under 16 you do not have to pay for prescriptions, dental or optical treatment. Once you are 16 you can still get free treatment if you are on income support or still in full-time education. If you are on YTS or earning you may still get some help because of your low income. Get the DSS leaflet AB11 *Help with NHS Costs* and form AG1 to claim, both from the Post Office. (The AG1 is a monster! If you need help completing it go to your local Citizen's Advice Bureau or Young People's Advisory Service.)

If you don't qualify for free or assisted treatment but you need frequent prescriptions then you can pay for your prescriptions in advance by buying a prescription 'passport' or 'season ticket'. These passports are for either £14.50 for four months or £40 for a year. Get form FP95 to claim, from your Post Office.

Pregnancy

If you become pregnant, one of your major worries will be telling your parents. This will be worse if you are under 16 as you may worry about your parents wanting to prosecute the man or boy concerned. However, you should not keep quiet merely because you are worried about a prosecution; your health is the first consideration. And generally the police will not be interested in prosecuting anyone if the man or boy concerned is less than two years older than you.

If your pregnancy has not been confirmed but is only a suspicion, try to find out one way or the other by going to the doctor or a clinic or using a pregnancy testing kit. If your period is only a week or two overdue the pregnancy kit may not be wholly reliable, but once you suspect that you are about 8–10 weeks late then a doctor will be able to tell by examining you, as well as by testing your urine.

Doctors should not disclose anything you tell them at the surgery (see Confidential advice from a doctor, above) although they will try to persuade you to tell your parents. If you do decide to do this, why not use another member of the family or another adult to act as a mediator? If you don't want to go to your doctor, try the local family planning clinic or a Brook Advisory Centre.

You will then have to make a number of important decisions, and a sympathetic doctor or advice agency will try to help you. If you decide to keep the baby instead of having an abortion, then a group like Life will give you advice and support. An agency like the Citizen's Advice Bureau will be able to give you additional information about housing and money. (See Chapter 7, When you decide to leave home.)

Abortion
If you decide to have an abortion then your doctor will know the local NHS arrangements. You will be able to have an abortion if the doctor believes that continuing the pregnancy:

1. Involves more risk to your life than having an abortion.
2. Is likely to involve more risk to your physical or mental health than having an abortion.
3. There is risk to other children.
4. There is the risk of mental or physical handicap to the unborn child.

Doctors are also able to take into account the social factors present in the woman's or girl's situation. This is where doctors might differ in their interpretation of the above conditions.

If a doctor is not prepared to agree to an abortion you might want to talk to one of the private clinics. Your local Citizen's Advice Bureau will know the names of private organisations who will help, counsel and carry out an abortion as well as giving post-operative support for the mother.

Whatever you decide make sure that it is your decision, not that of your parents, the father of the baby or your friends.

Contraception

If any young person, male or female, under the age of 16 wants contraceptive advice they should get it from a doctor, clinic or advice service. Doctors should advise you in confidence and will probably help you if they think you are mature enough to understand what you are doing. Try one of the advice agencies if you think that your doctor will not respect your confidence. Young men under 16 can always buy condoms from a chemist, but if they want free contraceptives from a family planning clinic they will be advised in the same way as a young girl under 16.

Once you are 16 you will be able to get advice from a doctor or clinic, without any restriction, on any aspect of contraception. Contraception given on prescription or by a family planning clinic is free. Some contraceptives such as the pill and condoms are available on prescription from your GP; others like caps and IUDs (the coil) can be fitted by doctors who have been trained to do so. The contraceptive sponge is available free from some Brook Advisory Clinics, but is very costly when bought at a chemist.

Drugs, alcohol and solvent abuse

If you take any prohibited drug, generally one you've obtained without medical help, then you have committed a criminal offence, as well as endangered your health.

If you want to stop taking any drug or give up any abuse such as excessive drinking or glue sniffing, go to any advice agency if you don't want to go to your doctor. See Useful addresses for groups who are prepared to help you.

MARRIAGE

Parental consent

Once you are 16 you can legally marry. However, until you are 18 you will need your parents' consent. If your parents are divorced or separated you will need the consent of the parent who has overall responsibility for you. If you wish to marry in the Church of England you do not have to have consent, but a vicar is unlikely to agree to marry you if he knows that your parents do not agree to the marriage.

If your parents do not agree to your marriage, then you can go to a magistrates court, a county court or the High Court and ask the court to overrule the decision, if you can convince them that your parents are being unreasonable. You will need to see a solicitor before going to court.

In extreme circumstances many young people have gone to Scotland, where you can marry at 16 without consent. Gretna Green is popular because it is one of the most southerly towns in Scotland. If you want to marry this way, you have to tell a district registrar of marriages in Scotland that you intend to marry. You will find their addresses and phone numbers in the Scottish telephone directories under Registration of births, deaths and marriages.

Living together

If you are under 16 and you go and live with someone of the same or the opposite sex, your parents will be able to convince the social services that you are at risk because you are below the age of consent (see Age of consent, below). Once you are 16 and you wish to live with someone, your parents can only stop you if they can convince a court that you are in danger. They may want to do this even if you go to live with someone of the same sex, or they feel any sexual relationship puts you in moral danger. This is apart from the fact that sexual acts between men are illegal until both are aged 21 years.

While there is no specific law which makes lesbianism illegal, if you are under 16 and your partner is over 16 your partner could be charged with indecent assault.

Also, if you read Chapter 7 you will see that leaving home can create all sorts of other difficulties.

SEX

Age of consent
It is an offence for a man to have sexual intercourse with a girl who is under the age of 16; the law says that she is unable to give consent and so will herself not be prosecuted.

A boy under the age of 14 is considered to be incapable of having sexual intercourse, but if he has sex with a girl under 16 he may be guilty of another offence such as indecent assault. Between the ages of 14 and 16 a boy can be charged with unlawful sexual intercourse; if convicted he could be sent to youth custody, detention centre or fined.

A girl cannot be prosecuted for unlawful sexual intercourse with men or boys at any age. However, if the boy is under 16 she could be charged with indecent assault, and if the boy concerned is under 14 then she could be charged with gross indecency.

Abuse
Abuse of young people and children takes place in different ways. They may be physically abused, beaten or hit repeatedly; neglected because their parents can't or won't look after them; deprived of affection; verbally bullied; or they may be sexually abused. All these are bound to affect how a young person behaves with their friends or the rest of their family. At first they may behave unusually – become aggressive, withdrawn or secretive, act younger than their actual age, not eat properly. In the long term it can create problems with sleeping, anxiety, feeling isolated and having a low opinion of oneself.

One of the most important things for someone who has been abused is finding someone who will believe them. Working up the courage to tell someone may take years; this is because people are frightened that they may break up the family, that the adult concerned will be taken away from them, that their mother or whoever they tell will not believe them. If you have been abused or one of your friends tells you that they have, remember this.

So who can you tell? Tell anyone you can trust – a teacher, a relative or a friend. If you just need to talk about it talk to one of the confidential help lines (see Useful addresses) or call the Samaritans (look in the phone book) or your local Citizen's Advice Bureau. None of these agencies will try to persuade you to do anything if you don't want to or are not yet ready to do anything.

Rape

An act of rape is committed when a man has unlawful sexual intercourse with a girl or woman who does not consent; in the eyes of the law there must be penetration of the vagina by the penis. However, rape crisis centres take a less restricted view and will talk to any woman or girl who has suffered an unpleasant sexual experience.

If you are raped you may not want to go to the police; in the past the police have not been seen as treating rape victims sympathetically. Also you may not feel prepared to go through all the process of identification, court appearances, etc. Talk to a friend or one of the support groups mentioned above before deciding.

If you decide to report the rape you will find that the police have in fact become more sensitive to the needs of rape victims. You will be interviewed by specially trained women police officers and hopefully examined by a woman doctor in an area of the police station especially set apart, not just an ordinary interview room. The police would prefer you to report the rape as soon after it has happened as possible and for you not to have bathed or changed your clothes, as evidence can be obtained from blood and semen which may help to identify the rapist.

Sexually transmitted diseases

If you contract a sexually transmitted disease such as a venereal disease (VD) or AIDS, advice and, in the case of VD, treatment will be available from your doctor or one of the special clinics attached to most NHS hospitals, both of whom should respect your confidence. While your privacy will be respected, the clinics will want to know the names of any sexual partners that you have had, in order that they may be traced and helped.

SOCIAL ACTIVITIES

Pubs and restaurants

1. If you are under 18 years of age you cannot buy alcohol from pubs, off licences or shops.
2. If you are under 14 you cannot go into a pub or any other licensed premises during opening hours, unless your parents own or run that establishment.
3. Once you are 14 you can go into a pub, but you cannot buy an alcoholic drink or have it bought for you.
4. Once you are 16 you can have wine, beer or cider, but not spirits, with a meal in a hotel or restaurant. Snack meals bought in a pub do not count, but if the pub has an area marked off as an eating area then you can drink there as long as you have a meal.

Regardless of your age a publican has the right to refuse to serve anyone in a pub. This does not just apply to young people who are apparently under age.

Smoking in public

You are allowed to smoke at any age, but it is illegal for a shopkeeper to sell you cigarettes, tobacco or cigarette papers if you are under 16, even if it is for someone else.

If you are under 16 and you are smoking in a public place you can have your cigarettes and tobacco confiscated by a park keeper or a policeman, but for some reason they cannot take your pipe or your tobacco pouch.

Cinema and videos

Films shown in cinemas are classified by the British Board of Film Censors; they make a decision about how suitable a film is for certain age groups, based on the subject of the film, language used and any scenes of violence or sex.They may insist that some scenes are cut or modifiedbefore they will issue a certificate, and films that are subsequently shown on television may have additional cuts in them as the television companies also have guidelines to follow when they are deciding about when to show a film.

The certificates that the British Board of Film Censors will issue are as follows:

1. U – suitable for all ages.
2. PG – parents may not wish their children to see this film as some of the scenes may be unsuitable, but unaccompanied children will be admitted.
3. 12 — no one under the age of 12 will be admitted.
4. 15 — no one under the age of 15 will be admitted.
5. 18 — no one under the age of 18 will be admitted.

In practice a cinema manager, like a publican, has discretion over whom they will admit. In most parts of the country children under five will not be admitted to a cinema unaccompanied; in London this applies to children under the age of 7.

Most videos are also classified:

1. Uc – universal, particularly suitable for children.
2. U – universal, suitable for all ages.
3. PG – parental guidance, some scenes may be unsuitable for children.
4. 15 – only suitable for people over 15, not to be supplied to anyone younger.
5. 18 – only suitable for people over 18, not to be supplied to anyone younger.

Gambling

1. If you are under 18 you are not allowed to go into or

place a bet in a betting shop, a gaming club or a bingo hall.

2. If you are under 16 you are allowed to win prizes, but not money, in bingo games at fairs and amusement arcades.
3. If you are under 16 you cannot buy tickets in a public lottery, but you can buy tickets in private raffles and lotteries, for example at a school or PTA fete.

WHEN YOU ARE 18

When you are 18 you can:

1. Vote in local, parliamentary and EEC elections.
2. Be called for jury service.
3. Make a will.
4. Act as an executor for someone's will.
5. Consent to an operation.
6. Donate blood.
7. Give your body to science (if you are 16 you may do this if your parents consent).
8. Apply for a passport without parental consent.
9. Leave home without parental consent.
10. Marry without parental consent.
11. Change your name without parental consent.
12. Trace your natural parents if you have been adopted.
13. Pay the community charge.
14. Buy and sell land, houses and flats, and apply for a mortgage.
15. Be sued and bring an action in court.
16. Sign contracts for hire purchase and credit agreements.
17. Pawn an article in a pawn shop.
18. Place a bet in a betting shop
19. See category 18 films.
20. Buy and sell alcohol.

But you must wait until you are 21 before you can stand as a candidate in both parliamentary and local elections or find that homosexual acts between consenting males are legal.

USEFUL
ADDRESSES

The following is only a selection of useful names and addresses.

GENERAL

Children's Legal Centre
20 Compton Terrace
London N1 2UN
071-359 6251

Childline
0800 1111
A free 24-hour confidential telephone line for children who are in trouble or in danger. It offers advice, support and practical help.

National Associaion of Citizen's Advice Bureaux
115–23 Pentonville Road
London N1 9LZ
071-833 2181
Or look in your phone book under Citizen's Advice Bureau. Provides free, confidential advice on all types of queries.

National Council for Civil Liberties
21 Tabard Street
London SE1 4LA
071-403 3888

National Youth Bureau
17–23 Albion Street
Leicester LE1 6GD
0533 471200
Provides information to those working with young people,
such as youth workers.

Just Ask
YMCA
112 Great Russell Street
London WC1
071-636 4308
Offers counselling and advice for young people. Telephone
number available 2–8 pm, Monday to Friday.

Justice for Children
35 Wellington Street
London WC2 7BN
071-836 5917

Association of Jewish Youth
50 Lindley Street
London E1 3AX
071-790 6407

Association of Muslim Youth
41 Gwendolen Road
Leicester
0533 730058

One Love Children's Centre
Coldharbour Works
245a Coldharbour Lane
London SW9
071-737 0446
For Rastafarian children under the age of 5.

National Association of Young People's Counselling Services

17–23 Albion Street
Leicester LE1 6GD
NAYPCAS is a national network drawing together information, advice and counselling organisations for young people. They will be able to refer you to a counselling organisation in your area.

WHEN YOU GO TO SCHOOL

Advisory Centre for Education

18 Victoria Park Square
London E2 9PB
081-980 4596

Brown Shipley Schools Insurance

Brown Shipley Insurance Services Ltd
52 Minories
London EC3
071-488 1450

Commission for Racial Equality

Elliot House
10–12 Arlington Street
London SW1E 5EH
071-828 7022

Dyslexia Institute

133 Gresham Road
Staines
Middlesex TW18 2AJ
Provides advice for parents and teachers of dyslexic children.

Education Otherwise
25 Common lane
Hemingford Abbots
Cambridge
0480 63130
Gives advice on educating children at home.

Equal Opportunities Commission
Overseas House
Quay Street
Manchester M3 3HN
061-833 9244

European Commission on Human Rights
Council of Europe
BP 431 R6
Strasbourg 67006 Cedex
France
010-33 88 61 49 61

WHEN THINGS GO WRONG IN THE FAMILY

National Stepfamily Association
162 Tenison Road
Cambridge CB1 2DP
0223 460312

National Association for Young People in Care (NAYPIC)
Second Floor
Maranar House
28–30 Mosley Street
Newcastle-upon-Tyne NE1 1DF
091 2612178
0274 728484/733134

Black and in Care
See NAYPIC, above.

A Voice for the Child in Care
60 Carysfort Road
Hornsey
London N8 8RB
081-348 2588

WHEN YOU WANT TO GET A JOB

The Princes Trust
8 Bedford Row
London WC1
071-430 0527
The Trust will make grants to groups and individual young people between the ages of 16-25 for self-help schemes and projects.

Youth Aid
9 Poland Street
London W1V 3DG
071-439 8523
Studies youth unemployment and publishes information to help the young unemployed.

WHEN YOU WANT TO TRAVEL

Joint Council for the Welfare of Immigrants
115 Old Street
London EC1V 9JR
071-251 8706

WHEN YOU GET INTO TROUBLE

Law Centres Federation
Duchess House
18–19 Warren Street
London W1P 5DB
071-387 8570

WHEN YOU DECIDE TO LEAVE HOME

The Advisory Service for Squatters
2 St Paul's Road
London N1
071-359 8814/5185, 12 pm to 6 pm

Alone in London
West Lodge
190 Euston Road
London NW1 2EF
071-387 6184
Offers advice and support to young homeless people
between 16–21 in London.

Centrepoint
33 Long Acre
London WC2 9LA
071-379 3466
Runs a night-shelter for young people and a long-term
support hostel. Also lets flats and bedsits to young people
for fair rents.

Leaving Home Project
5 Egmont House
115 Shaftesbury Avenue
London W1V 7DJ
071-437 2068
To increase public knowledge of the problems of leaving
home, especially among the young.

Shelter – National Campaign for the Homeless
88 Old Street
London EC1V 9HU
071-253 0202

WHEN YOU CAN DECIDE FOR YOURSELF

Lesbian and Gay Youth Movement
BM/GYM
London WC1N 3XX
081-317 9690

National Association for Welfare of Children in Hospital
Argyle House
29–31 Euston Road
London NW1
071-833 2041

Young Group of Gamblers Anonymous
Abbey Community Centre
29 Marsham Street
London SW1
071-352 3060

British Pregnancy Advisory Service (BPAS)
Austy Manor
Wooton Wawen
Solihull
West Midlands B95 6BX
05642 3225
To help and advise women facing an unwanted pregnancy. Services include pregnancy testing, contraception, male and female sterilisation and infertility help.

Brook Advisory Services
153a East Street
London SE17 2SD
071-708 1234/1390
Gives advice on contraception and sexual problems.

Life (Save the Unborn Child)
118–20 Warwick Street
Leamington Spa
Warwicks CV32 4QY
0926 21587/311667
To help women avoid abortion by offering counselling and
help. Also housing through Life Care and Housing Trust.

Rape crisis centres
There is a rape crisis centre in most major towns and
cities in the UK. Your local Citizen's Advice Bureau can
tell you which is your nearest, but if you have difficulty
telephone one of the 24 hour telephone lines in London or
Birmingham:

London 071-837 1600
Birmingham 021-233 2122/2455

Rape crisis centres provide a free, confidential service to
anyone who has been forced into a sexual act without their
consent. They prefer the woman or girl to call herself
when she feels the need to and not because she has been
made to.

Release
c/o 347a Upper Street
London N1 0PD
071-289 1123
071-603 8654 (24 hours)
Gives advice on drugs and legal problems.

Teen Challenge UK
Teen Challenge Centre
Penygroes Road
Gorslas
Llanelli
Dyfed
0269 842718
Practical and positive help for young people with drug,
solvent and alcohol abuse.

USEFUL
PUBLICATIONS

Voluntary Agencies Directory, Bedford Square Press – every Citizen's Advice Centre has a copy.

Education Yearbook, Longman, London – can be found in your local reference library.

Education Rights Handbook, available from the Children's Legal Centre, 20 Compton Terrace, London N1 2UN.

The following leaflets provide further useful information about available benefits:

CH1   *Child Benefit*
FB23   *Young Peoples' Guide to Social Security*
FB8   *Babies and Benefits*
FB27   *Bringing up Children*
SB20   *A Guide to Income Support*

INDEX

129

INDEX

squatting, 96
statementing, 21
statements, police, 74-75
step-parents, 34-35
students and benefit, 103-105
supervised activity order, 84
supervision order, 45, 83
suspension, from school, 13-14

tape recordings, 75
terms and conditions, 56
trains, 64
transport, to school, 17
travel, 63-67
truancy, 12

Underground, 63
uniform, 11

veneral disease, 116
videos, 117
Visual Display Units (VDUs), 19
voluntary care, 42

weapons, 3
wills, 109
work *see* employment

Youth Training Scheme, 61-62, 100

132

All Optima books are available at your bookshop or newsagent, or can be ordered from the following address:

Optima, Cash Sales Department,
PO Box 11, Falmouth, Cornwall TR10 9EN

Please send cheque or postal order (no currency), and allow 60p for postage and packing for the first book, plus 25p for the second book and 15p for each additional book ordered up to a maximum charge of £1.90 in the UK.

Customers in Eire and BFPO please allow 60p for the first book, 25p for the second book plus 15p per copy for the next 7 books, thereafter 9p per book.

Overseas customers please allow £1.25 for postage and packing for the first book and 28p per copy for each additional book.